Exploring Parish Churches in Northamptonshire

Compiled & Edited by Tony Noble
Research by John & Vera Worledge

JEMA PUBLICATIONS

Published 1999 by Jema Publications
© Tony Noble, John & Vera Worledge
ISBN: 1-871468-93-0

Publisher's Note

Every care has been taken in the preparation of this
book. The publishers cannot accept responsibility
for any inaccuracies or for any loss, damage or
inconvenience resulting from the use of this book.

Front Cover photograph: Stained glass window, Cosgrove Church
Back Cover photographs: Starting top left clockwise, Pitsford,
Hartwell, Sutton Bassett and Sywell.

Designed by David Joyce of
The Design MAP 01604 231236

JEMA PUBLICATIONS
40 Ashley Lane
Moulton
Northampton

CONTENTS

Acknowledgements		vi
Northamptonshire Map		vii
Introduction		viii
Northampton		11
Stoke Bruerne and Towcester		17
Brackley and the South-West		26
Daventry and the Heights		43
Rockingham Forest, Corby and Kettering		61
The Nene Valley		76
Wellingborough and Surrounding Villages		88
Appendix 1	Glossary	101
Appendix 2	Features to Look for in an Old Church	103
Appendix 3	Periods of English Architecture	104
Bibliography		105
Index		107

ACKNOWLEDGMENTS

Very many people have helped to create this book and our thanks are due to all of them. In particular we would like to thank the following for allowing us to use their illustrations Pam Borley, Mrs Chapman, Peter Coleman, JR Cox, Mandy Dawkins, Carl Johnson, Maurice Johnson, Mr Marsden, John Neville, Allan Powell, Robert Swinford, Colin Tidbury, Robert Walls, Mrs Viney, the Rector and PCC of Newnham, Norton and Denford parish churches and to Ron Wilson, Head of Everdon Field Studies Centre. Our thanks also go to many of the parish churches who have allowed us to use their church history booklets for information and to Colin Lindsay for help and advice. John and Vera thank many of the lovely village people whom they met during their research and with whom they shared interesting village anecdotes. Finally if we have inadvertently failed to mention someone who has contributed we do apologise.

John, Vera and Tony
November 1999

MAPS

THIS BOOK IS DEDICATED TO THE LATE JOHN T NEVILLE RIBA

NORTHAMPTONSHIRE

1 Northampton - p11

2 Stoke Bruerne and Towcester - p17

3 Brackley and the South West - p26

4 Daventry and the Heights - p43

5 Rockingham Forest, Corby and Kettering - p61

6 The Nene Valley - p76

7 Wellingborough and Surrounding Villages - p88

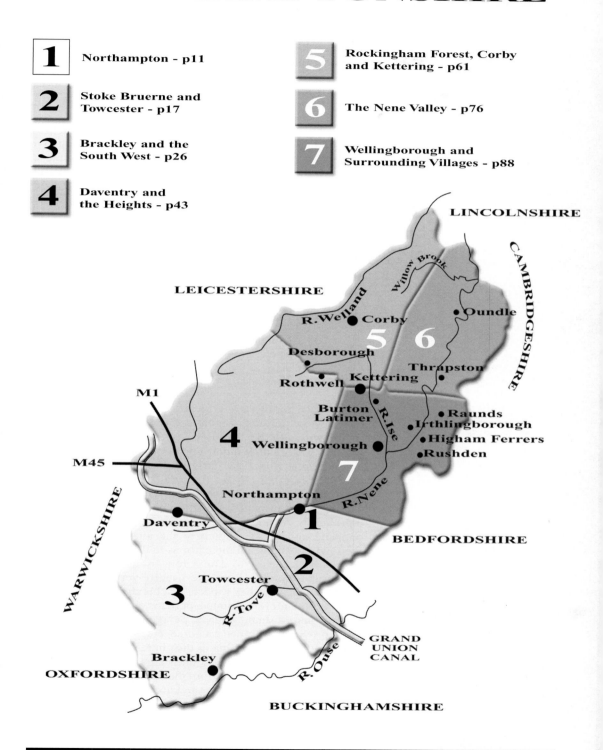

INTRODUCTION

Most of us are inquisitive. We often look curiously around seeking an explanation for the unknown. Church architecture is an absorbing study and, with increased knowledge, a greater understanding and enjoyment of the wonderful heritage within our churches can be had. Before describing over two hundred and fifty of Northamptonshire's treasures a brief introduction as to what to look for, and where, will, we hope, make your explorations more worthwhile and interesting. Also refer to the appendix for further help in understanding the terminology used. We have attempted to group the churches into areas, this has been a difficult task, especially near to an area division, and whilst almost all Northamptonshire's churches have been mentioned there will be the occasional one that is missing. Any future reprint will attempt to correct this.

The periods of church architecture can be roughly divided into eight headings:

Saxon	AD600 to 1100
Norman	1066 to 1190
Transitional	Norman to Early English
Early English	1200 to 1300
Decorated	1280 to 1350
Perpendicular	1350 to 1550
Classical	1600 to 1799
Victorian	1800 to 1900

There is, naturally, some overlapping and churches will have several periods of architecture within their structure. There will also be common styles within a period, for instance a Norman window and door have a familiar semi-circular arch, whilst the Early English windows and doors have a pointed arch. During the Decorated and Perpendicular periods, doors and windows become more elaborate and ornamental with the decorated arch becoming slightly flatter. The church font, usually found at the opposite end of the church to the altar and towards the west, will also give an indicator as to the age of the church. Normally it is easy to date a font by its appearance. The Saxon and Norman fonts are usually very plain and like stone tubs. Like other aspects of church architecture they then became more decorated, perhaps on a decorated plinth and a different shape - maybe octagonal. Later fonts were often provided with decorated covers, sometimes made of oak. Look for the piscina in the church. This is a form of drain, usually found in the south wall of the sanctuary. This was used to take rinsings from the sacred vessels, the water running out into the consecrated ground of the churchyard.

Screens are important in a church. Many early screens were between the nave, where the people sit, and the chancel, where the choir and clergy are. This was especially so during medieval times. The rood screen, with the rood beam over the top, would often have the figures of Mary, the mother of Jesus, and St. John on either side of Christ on the cross, called the 'rood'. Steps can often be found either side of the chancel rood screen. These led up to the rood beam and loft. Many old pews had bench ends often carved with figures, animals or a family coat of arms. In some churches you will find misericords in the choir stalls. These are hinged or tip up seats and during long services, when clergy had to stand, they provided support. These were very popular during the medieval period.

Sedilia (a group of three seats let into the wall of the south chancel), pews, roofs, memorials, towers and many more will all tell a story and give a date, and no two churches will be the same.

So go out and explore your churches and I am sure that you will be surprised with your findings.

ST RUMBOLD'S, STOKE DOYLE

Northampton

The County town sits on the north bank of the River Nene and the Saxons first settled on the site, probably around AD650.

The Vikings then came and ransacked the town, which was rebuilt by the Normans. The churches suffered during this period and the Holy Sepulchre is probably the oldest building, dating from 1100 and the best preserved of the four remaining round churches in the country. St Peter's and All Saints both had early Saxon churches on their sites, only to be destroyed and then rebuilt by the Normans. Sadly All Saints suffered from the Great Fire of Northampton in 1675 and had to be rebuilt again.

J.R.COX

All Saint's Church,
at the centre of Northampton's busiest thoroughfare.

he town of Northampton has many churches of contrasting architecture. **ALL SAINTS CHURCH** sits imposingly on an island in the centre of Northampton's busiest thoroughfare. Although it was almost certain that the earliest church here was Saxon, this was destroyed by the Danes in AD1010. A Norman church built during the eleventh century by Simon de St Liz, Earl of Northampton was largely destroyed in 1675 by the great fire of Northampton, so the building largely dates from this period. There is some Norman stone within the structure of the four large pillars supporting the tower, which is itself largely medieval. The tower and the crypt, which is below the chancel, were the only parts of the church to have survived the fire. During the thirteenth and fourteenth centuries Parliament met regularly in the castle of Northampton and the clergy of the Province of Canterbury met in All Saints church. The chancel, like much of the church, is mainly seventeenth century. All the important civic services are held here. Look for the carved and gilded mayor's seat (1680) on the right of the centre aisle. Before leaving the church climb the stairs to the gallery to appreciate more fully the grand and magnificent dome.

Leaving the church you will pass through the portico which was added in 1701. The ionic columns reflect the style of the ancient Greek and Roman buildings - typical of the Classical period. Look back to the magnificent statue above the portico. It represents King Charles II in a Roman tunic and was erected during the reign of Queen Anne. This was in memory of the King who decreed that a thousand tons of timber, obtained from the Royal forests, should be made available to help rebuild the church after the great fire. In remembrance of Charles, Northampton used to hold a procession on Oak Apple Day, 29 November, but now the custom is to place an oak wreath garland on the statue.

Another of Simon de St Liz's churches was the round church of the **HOLY SEPULCHRE,** also built in Northampton. It is now one of only four left in England and is probably the largest and best preserved. It was built after St Liz had returned from his first crusade in 1099 and as a thanksgiving offering for his safe return. His design was modelled on the Holy Sepulchre in Jerusalem and consisted of the Round part of the church and the straight chancel leading east. The chancel now forms the nave and the remainder of the church has been added to over the years, but much of the original Norman church is there for everyone to explore and enjoy.

There is an overwhelming feeling immediately entering the church. An expectant air as you step down into the 'Round' and become surrounded by eight massive circular Norman pillars. The capital head of each one is different. Immediately to the right of the porch and a few yards along is a tall narrow niche. This cuts through an original Norman window and the arch can be seen quite clearly. Enter the nave through the central of the three sets of steps and immediately to your left and beside the Kerr monument is part of one of the Norman windows of the old chancel. Above this are also six crude but detailed carvings, dated the fifteenth century, of musicians with their instruments. Can you spot the organ, kettle drums, panpipes, bagpipe, rebec (like a violin) and an organistrum (an organ where the keys are pressed with the right hand and the handle turned with the left)?

Move across to the south aisle, which was built during the fourteenth century, and stand by the piscina. Look up towards the nave roof and you will see several Norman corbels which originally helped to hold up the Norman chancel. There are a large number of military memorials and relics around the church. This is because the Holy Sepulchre became the garrison church of the former Northamptonshire Regiment and their memorial chapel of St George is in the south aisle. Several windows in the church have been given by the Regiment in memory of comrades killed in battle. Perhaps the most notable one is the west window in the north aisle. This is known as the 'Battle Window' and it shows Richard I, on his third crusade, at the Battle of Jaffa in 1192. This window may well be unique in its content. From the north aisle, and looking up to the nave roof, you can see Norman corbels, similar to those on the south side and seen earlier. Like the others, these were probably in the original Norman chancel. As you leave the church look at the scratch dial on the left and just above head height. This stone is not a sundial but was used as a mass dial, which showed the time of the church service. The stone probably dates from the ninth century and is on the site of a former church.

Finally, spend time to look at the outside of the church. On the west side of the porch there is a recess in the outer wall and, although normally these are used for tombs, this particular one seems unused. Above the recess is an original Norman window. Walk around to the west side of the tower and find the pitted bullet marks at about head height on the buttresses. These probably occurred during the Civil War.

Whether you stand and admire the exterior tower of **ST PETER'S, NORTHAMPTON,** with its pyramid shaped point, sitting like a skull cap on top of the Norman tower and surrounded by seventeenth century battlements, or the ornamental carved arches inside the church, your admiration and joy will make your visit inspirational. Built in AD1160 by Simon de St Liz (probably the grandson of Simon, the builder of the Holy Sepulchre) and on the site of an original Saxon church, the exterior rugged walls of the aisles have many Norman arches. This is also a characteristic of the tower, which, although retaining much of its Norman character, was rebuilt in the early seventeenth century. Entering the church from the north door and through the Norman arches, the immediate impact is one of utter amazement. The decorative arcading on the nave arches and the pier carvings is fabulous. Investigate the capitals of the columns and find carved heads, foliage, animals and winged creatures. Of particular interest is the mystery carving, on the west face of the capital of the middle pier of the south arcade. No explanation has yet been given as to why the human figure has its face looking out, with the rest of its body turned inwards. See the backs of the hands and ribs.

Further evidence of the Norman origin of the church probably comes from the tall columns (piers) on which rest the arches. Look closely to find the arches resting alternately on single columns and on tall piers with additional supports. These taller central columns could have been used to support either a flat roof or arches which crossed the nave. These larger columns rest on Norman bases, which means that if these were inside the Norman church then the actual church was under these columns.

Stand at the furthest point east in the chancel and look towards the tower. Admire the decorated Norman shaped arch leading through to the tower and the octagonal fourteenth century font. The outer walls are mainly of the Decorated period with the sanctuary (housing the High Altar) restored in the mid nineteenth century. Leave the church through the north door, but before venturing into the busy Northampton streets look at the tower which is supported at the west corners by round buttresses in clusters of three. This style is extremely unusual. Finally notice the plaque on the church railings which informs the reader of the historical associations and archaeological findings in the area. The plaque reads:

SAXON ORIGINS AND ST. PETER'S CHURCH.
ST. PETER'S CHURCH IS ONE OF THE FINEST EXAMPLES OF NORMAN
ARCHITECTURE IN THE COUNTRY. ERECTED AROUND 1170 BY SIMON DE
ST LIZ, FIRST NORMAN EARL OF NORTHAMPTON, ON THE SITE OF AN
EARLIER SAXON CHURCH. CLOSE BY ARCHEOLOGICAL EXCAVATIONS
REVEALED THAT THIS WAS THE SITE OF AN EARLY SAXON SETTLEMENT
(ABOUT 400-650AD). IMPORTANT MID-SAXON FINDS INDICATE THAT
THIS WOULD BE THE ORIGINAL HAMTUN SETTLEMENT, A CENTRE OF
SOME IMPORTANCE BEING A ROYAL ESTATE THAT GREW INTO AN
IMPORTANT DANISH TOWN ABOUT 900AD.

ST MATTHEW'S CHURCH, along the Kettering Road in Northampton, had its foundation stone laid in 1891 and was consecrated in 1893. The church spire rises to a height of one hundred and seventy feet and dominates the surrounding streets. Having visited many small churches, St. Matthews by any standards is very large and spacious. Music plays an important part in the life of the church. It is the home of the Northampton Bach Choir and the church with its fine organ, minstrel gallery and considerable size provide an ideal situation for their concerts. The church is also famous for two modern pieces of art. One is Henry Moore's famous *Madonna and Child* which was sculpted in 1943/44 and is best seen from the pulpit. Look at the effective way the stone's natural colours are used and the dignity and gracefulness obtained by the artist. Contrast this with Graham Sutherland's *Crucifixion* found on the opposite south wall. The violence and starkness of the subject is vividly portrayed, showing the grey Christ on the cross, against a sharply contrasting mauve background. If you are an admirer of Sutherland's work, remember his tapestry of *Christ in Glory* at Coventry Cathedral. It is worth visiting St Matthew's just to see this painting.

Pam Barley ©97

KINGSTHORPE, once a village but now a suburb of Northampton, Kingsthorpe is about one and a half miles from the centre and along the Market Harborough road. **ST JOHN THE BAPTIST** with an embattled tower supporting a lofty spire was first built during the Norman period and added to in the thirteenth century (1200-1300, Early English). The windows above the arcades in the nave and in the chancel are Norman and there may even have been a church here during the Saxon period. There are Norman pillars carved with 'nailhead' ornamentation and the capitals of the pillars are rich in Norman foliage. In the course of restoration work, a number of monumental crosses and fragments of other memorials were found and these were set in the walls of the choir vestry under the tower or in the east wall of the clergy vestry. There are also fragments of medieval work in some of the carved ends, or poppy heads of the choir stalls. Look for a mermaid, the head of a monk, a frog and a lion. The pulpit is Jacobean and the oak chest near the vestry bears the date 1708. It was during the restoration in 1863 that the present oak pews were installed and both altars are modern, 1957 and 1966. The fourteenth century crypt can only be entered from the outside of the church and the only light in the crypt comes from two windows in the east and south wall. A report dated 1863 states that when the crypt was cleared out a number of human bones were found.

DUSTON. There are two churches in the village, the more modern one being built to meet the needs of an expanding suburb of Northampton. The older **ST LUKE'S CHURCH** stands on high ground giving extensive views of Northampton. It is a beau-

tiful building with strong Early English and Gothic architecture. We enter through a Norman doorway and are taken aback by the way the church is laid out, for we

have an altar in the usual position, the east end, but there is also an altar at the west end of the church. This has been done to accommodate the increasing congregations. If the service is held at the east end then only about thirty people can see the altar owing to the massive pillars that support the tower, which is in the centre of the church, so when there is a large congregation the service is held at the west end to allow greater participation.

The church is worth exploring so spend a while looking and investigating. Close to the west altar is a Norman pillar and a wonderful statue called *"The Dancing Madonna"*. The inner doorway of the south porch is Norman; look for the fourteenth century corbals supporting the old chancel roof, they are the figures of musicians with their instruments - a kettle drum, harp, a viol and bagpipes. The Norman theme continues with a large fluted font.

Look for the leper's squint, below left, put there enabling lepers to watch the services without coming into contact

with the congregation. Explore the churchyard and find a very unusual tomb, a great slab of stone surmounted by an enormous anchor, said to be the grave of a very wealthy gentleman who owned the local quarries and who was a yachtsman with the Royal Yacht Squadron.

Also the skull and crossbone tombstone, top right.

ABINGTON. Once a village but now a close suburb of Northampton the church of **ST PETER and ST PAUL** stands in the park, which together with the house was once part of Abington Abbey!

The church was rebuilt in 1821 after it had suffered storm damage, although the earlier church dates from the Norman and medieval periods with the lower part of the tower remaining. Elizabeth Barnard, grand-daughter and last descendant of William Shakespeare lived in the Manor House, which is now a museum and is buried in the churchyard. There are various memorials in the church, some to the Barnards and others to the Thursbys who succeeded the Barnards as owners of the manor.

DALLINGTON, another suburb of Northampton and approximately one and a half miles north west from the centre has the church of **ST MARY** built during the twelfth to fourteenth centuries, but again like many churches added to over the years. The church has a

Norman doorway and a thirteenth century tower with a curious small Saxon fragment in the inner north wall. The church has many memorials to the Raynsford family who owned estates in Dallington. In 1673 Lord Chief Justice Raynsford built and endowed the almshouses on the green and the north chapel known as the Raynsford chapel was built in 1679. Another well known local figure Sir Joseph Jekyll, Master of the Rolls, who bought the estate from the Raynsfords, had Dallington Hall built during the eighteenth century. Sir Joseph (1752) and his wife's (1766) memorial is in the church. The font is octagonal and bears the arms of the Raynsford's.

ST GILES CHURCH is probably best known for its monument to Robert Brown, who was founder of the Brownist movement later called the Congregational Church and part of the Nonconformist religion. He is buried in the churchyard and his monument is found on the south side of this most charming of Northampton's churchyards. Robert Brown is thought to have been born about 1550 and after preaching against the Church of England he wandered the country until he finally settled in Northampton. He studied Divinity at Cambridge and after settling in the county he accepted the rectory at Thorpe Achurch in 1590. Rather strange this, as the Bishop of Peterborough had excommunicated him. Perhaps Browne changed his mind! Unfortunately he died in Northampton Gaol in 1630, after failing to pay his parish rate - a sad end to a man who had a deep, sincere faith and belief in his movement.

St Giles Church itself occupies a site immediately within the old wall of the town and on the eastern side. It had to be partly rebuilt in 1616 after the original Norman tower had collapsed during a storm in 1613. This destroyed part of the nave and left much of the church insecure. Initially the church, a cross shape, was constructed around the beginning of the twelfth century without aisles, and these together with the lengthening of the church were added later. The fine Norman west door was taken down and reconstructed during extensive nineteenth century enlargements of the church.

© David Twigger 1999

You enter **ST PETER'S, WESTON FAVELL** through a Norman doorway and there is further Norman evidence with the round arch in the west wall and the lower part of the tower. The tower once had a spire but this was destroyed by lightning on the 19 May 1726. The chancel was added during the thirteenth century and there are still the original lancet windows under an arch in the south wall. Look to see the beautifully embroidered altar cloth depicting the last supper. This is supposed to date from 1698. A new modern vestry has been added and this village suburb of Northampton now has substantial new housing.

Stoke Bruerne & Towcester

The open countryside south-east of Northampton is shattered by three main transport routes. The M1 motorway, the railway and the A5 Watling Street, all carrying immense daily traffic, in stark contrast to the Grand Union Canal, now only used for leisure. The churches in the area are scattered far and wide, many are close to Watling Street, which two thousand years ago would have echoed to the tramp of the Roman Legions, marching north from London to Chester. Towcester was an important fort and staging post. When the Romans left churches were developed by the Saxons and Normans and there is much evidence in the area of their activity.

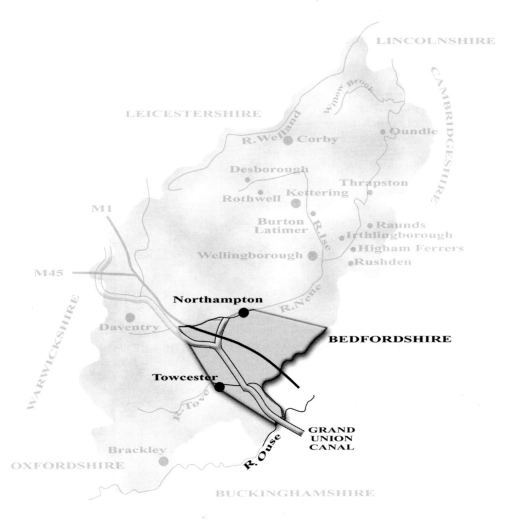

ISLINGBURY is situated just outside of Northampton along the A45 Daventry road and on the south bank of the River Nene. **ST LUKES** was built from Northamptonshire ironstone around 1330 and is a fine example of Early English through to Decorated architecture. Look for the fifteenth century scratch dial on the south wall and the fine gargoyles at the corner of the chancel on the exterior wall. There are more gargoyles and corbels both around the outside and in the nave arcades, the chancel arch and with the sedilia and piscina. The beautiful east window depicts the people of the Second World War and was presented to the church by the Dunkley family in memorial to their son who fell at El-Alemein in 1942. Whilst looking in the chancel see the beautiful three sedilia seat.

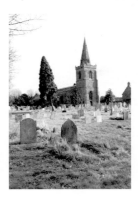

ST MICHAEL'S, UPTON dates back to the Norman times but there may have been a Saxon building on the site or close by before. Evidence of the Norman period is the odd Norman windows and the north and south doorways, whilst a Saxon building, possibly of the sixth or seventh century was excavated west of the church in 1965. There is a memorial to Sir Richard Knightley and his wife, made before his death. The Knightleys owned Upton Hall (now Quinton School), for almost two hundred years from 1419. Sadly St Michael's is one of the county's redundant churches.

ST MICHAEL'S CHURCH, BUGBROOKE with its spire dominates the old village and is perhaps best known for its beautiful fifthteenth century wooden rood screen with a canopy, perhaps one of only a few surviving in the county. The fanvaulted canopy has superb window tracery and exquisite hanging roses. The church was largely built during the thirteenth

and fourteenth centuries, but it is likely that the nave is Norman as it has four pointed arches in the south arcade supported by Norman columns. There are some lovely stained glass windows and memorials to explore in the church.

ST PETER AND ST PAUL, NETHER HEYFORD was built during the thirteenth and fourteenth centuries. The tower and the chancel have medieval heads around them and the nave has arches from this period, together with carved corbels of stone heads, shields and angels for the roofs of the aisles. The font, like many others, has leaf carvings but interestingly has been painted by the medieval artist, although this is now fading. Look for the lovely monument to Sir Walter Mauntell and his wife. Sir Walter died in 1467.

At the time of writing **FLORE** sits on the very busy A45 hopefully awaiting a bypass. **ALL SAINTS**, left, is situated on the edge of the village and was built in the soft brown Northamptonshire stone mainly during the Early English (thirteenth century) and the following fourteenth century. The huge tower was built during this period and interestingly the chancel is not in line with the nave. The doors in the tower are reputed to be around 600 years old and the sixteenth century barrel shaped font has a unusual history. It was thrown out of the church and spent a long time in the fields as a cattle trough, eventually it was rescued and taken into Dodford church and then brought back to All Saints. Look around the font for remnants of a staple which was used to lock the font from witches. These are often found on fonts and indicative of this superstition. Also look at the east window in the south aisle for the heroic story of Bruce Capell. His wooden cross brought home from Flanders by an officer hangs on the wall. He was only 22 years of age and he was awarded the Military Cross for his heroism on the battlefields of Flanders. Other memorials are found around the church.

ROTHERSTHORPE, now close to the motorway used to be a quiet village but all this has changed - there is even a motorway service station named after the village. Bury Close in the village is built on an ancient earthwork and the village is situated on the old pre-historic routeway, The Jurassic Way. There may have been a church on the current site as far back as the seventh century as there has been found the base of an old preaching cross. Certainly the current church has Norman origins with a font from that period. The church of **ST PETER AND ST PAUL** is now mainly thirteenth and fourteenth centuries with the tower and its unusual saddleback roof, arcades, chancel arches,

windows and the south doorway all from these periods. Look around for the head of a wheeled cross, it stands three feet high and has the carving of the crucifixion with flowers and foliage. It is said that it was found in 1869 when they demolished a barn in the village and a cross head like this is very rare.

A few miles from Northampton and just off the A43 Towcester road is the village of **GAYTON**, probably more important for the Grand Union Canal and the marina - Gayton Basin. The church of **ST MARY** dates back to the Norman period and has a tower, the base of which is Norman with the upper part nineteenth century. The rest of the church is Early English and of the Decorated period of architecture. There is much to see and explore in the church. The circular font is Norman or is a good replica, whilst the carved misericords are superb. See if you can find carvings of a lion, dragon, female figures and Jesus' Entry into Jerusalem? The reredos has linenfold carving. Look also to find another rare wooden effigy; it is Sir Philip de Gayton who died in 1316, he lies on a lavish tomb in his full armour and sword, with his dog at his feet. In the north aisle there is a recess in which lies a lady, reputedly to be Scholastica de Gayton of 1354 and above her lies an infant, she is Mabila de Murdak and was a grand daughter of Sir Phillip. Her mother, 'a de Gayton', is said to have been burnt at the stake for murdering her husband.

MILTON MALSOR on the old A43 Towcester road and now bypassed, has a church dedicated to the **HOLY CROSS** and is known for its beautifully carved Decorated 'wheel' window at the end of the south aisle. There appears to have been a lot of restoration work during the nineteenth century, although the oldest part of the church are the round pillars in the north arcade which date from 1180-90 and the church was initially erected during the 1350 to 1450 period. Look for the narrow blocked up priest's doorway in the south chapel, left, and the twelfth century font.

COURTEENHALL is a small village consisting of a few houses and lying about five miles from Northampton and close to the M1 motorway. The church of **ST PETER AND ST PAUL** was built largely during the Early English and Decorated periods and although restored does retain fabric from this period. The south doorway may even be earlier but many of the arches and arcades come from the main period of building. Look for the ogee heads on the sedilia and piscina, the recently restored leper's window and the wall paintings on the west pier of the south arcade, showing the upper halves of female figures. Courteenhall has long been the home of the Wake family and there are memorials in the church to the family. Perhaps the strangest one being the table tomb to Sir Richard Ousley's family who married into the Wake family through his second wife and whose strange inscription runs around the stone tomb. There is also an imposing marble monument with two kneeling effigies to Sir Samuel Johns and his wife Mary, he was the founder of the Grammar School and the memorial shows both with their hands held to their hearts.

QUINTON village lying close to the motorway and south of Northampton has both Roman and Saxon origins close by. The church of **ST JOHN THE BAPTIST** dates back to the Normans although there may have been a church here earlier. There is a late Norman pointed lancet window in the west wall and the south-west quoin. The west tower was added in the thirteenth century, prior to this the church finished with the nave. The whole church was remodelled in 1801 but retains three bays and piers and the chancel arch from the earlier period.

PRESTON DEANERY, close to Piddington village has a church now in the care of the Redundant Churches. **ST PETER AND ST PAUL** was sadly unused for over fifty years during the sixteenth century and a local squire sold the lead and bells and started dismantling the church. It was restored during the following century and still retains several Norman features. The west tower and chancel arch are Norman with a round-headed doorway in the chancel dated around twelve hundred.

PIDDINGTON lies close to the motorway and just off the A50 Newport Pagnell road. The church of **ST JOHN THE BAPTIST** was probably built around the thirteenth century and the strange looking tower was built during this period and the following century. The tower was built in three stages and the spire rises out of a variety of windows and pinnacles. Inside the church, which is entered through a thirteenth century doorway are eight medieval arches and clerestory windows. The font is also thirteenth century. In the south aisle is an ancient piscina and five superb carved cherubs.

ST MARY'S CHURCH, HORTON, situated a few miles from Northampton, has as its claim to fame a direct connection with William the Conqueror. His niece, the Countess Judith, owned the parish of Horton and Yardley. There was probably a church here in Saxon times but the present one was built during the Norman period. The other royal connection is with Henry VIII. There is a quite remarkable alabaster altar tomb occupying the centre of the chancel. This tomb is in memory of the uncle and aunt of Catherine Parr, the sixth wife of Henry VIII. Sir William Parr had married into the Salisbury family, who owned the Horton estate, and he later became

Lord Parr of Horton. The figures around the side of the tomb are called 'weepers' and represent grieving members of the family. Yet another memorial to a family who owned the estate! Sadly the church is now thought to be unsafe and has been closed, the east window having been removed for safe keeping, and a fund has been started to raise a substantial amount to repair the church. The parishioners travel to Piddington for worship.

ST GEORGE'S CHURCH, WOOTTON sits on a knoll in the village. It consists of a nave, north and south aisles, chancel and Perpendicular embattled tower. The church was built during the thirteenth century and has been extensively restored in 1844 and again in 1865. Little of the original church remains - in the chancel is a lancet window, three arcades and the north and south doors are all from the original building. On removing the plaster during the 1844 repairs, two very ancient paintings were found in the chancel and on the wall in the south aisle look for a medieval bracket carved with the figure of a man with long hair.

COLLINGTREE village situated very close to the M1 motorway is dedicated to **ST COLUMBA**, who founded the monastery on the Island of Iona off the north-east coast of England. Indeed to have a church named after this saint away from the north of England is a rarity. Looking at evidence the church was probably originally late Norman and Early English. There is a blocked Norman doorway and close by a recess with a Norman arch. The round font with carvings of a head and monster is probably thirteenth century. Although restored over the years, and especially in the nineteenth century, the south doorway and the south arcades  and piers are from the early period. Developments continued during the medieval period with a tall tower arch, a wide chancel arch and three sedilia and their mouldings. The church is the proud owner of several sixteenth century books and much of the stained glass is modern, being put into the windows during the Victorian period, probably during the restorations.

ROADE on the main A508 Northampton to Milton Keynes road, and although the church of **ST MARY** is Norman, like many of our churches has been altered and restored during the seventeenth and nineteenth century. There is a Norman south doorway and two of the chancel windows are also Norman, together with the round font. The tower is thirteenth century and perhaps, because it is close to Courteenhall, the home of the Wake family we find a medieval unlettered table top tomb in which it is said lies Richard Wake and his two wives.

ASHTON village, near Roade, must not to be confused with the Ashton of World Conker Championships fame which is near Oundle. **ST MICHAEL'S** medieval church, definitely worth exploring, has a most unusual and rare saddle-back tower built during the fourteenth century. There is a Norman circular tub-shaped font and a rare chestnut wood carving of a local knight, Philip the Wolf, who, it is said, fought alongside Edward I (1239-1307). This wooden carving is one of less than a hundred surviving in the country. The battered fourteenth century carving with hands clasped in prayer and minus one foot lies resting on a stone tomb. An old alabaster monument of a knight, also of the same age as the wooden carving, lies close by. Finally, and continuing the artistic theme there are several imposing brasses dedicated to Robert Marriot and his family.

ST JOHN THE BAPTIST, HARTWELL was built in 1851 but materials and architectural characteristics were included from the older Norman building. As you enter

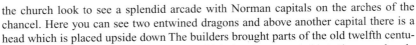

Below: St John the Baptist, Hartwell, depicting the double bell cote and Norman door carvings.

the church look to see a splendid arcade with Norman capitals on the arches of the chancel. Here you can see two entwined dragons and above another capital there is a head which is placed upside down The builders brought parts of the old twelfth century church, including the arches, which they incorporated into the new church. The old church sat in the fields, close to where Chapel Farm is today and away from the village, and it was felt that it was too far for the parishioners to walk.

BLISWORTH, situated between Northampton and Towcester is now quiet since the A43 bypass was built, but to stroll along Church Lane and then into the church is like walking into the eighteenth and nineteenth centuries with their old thatched cottages. The church of **ST JOHN THE BAPTIST** was largely built during the thirteenth to sixteenth centuries with later restorations. There are the original rood screen stairs and large brown tablets either side of the altar on which are written the 'Ten Commandments' from Exodus 10. An altar tomb in the south aisle is to Roger and Elizabeth Wake. Roger Wake was sheriff of the county in 1483 and died in 1504. His widow lived a further sixty one years dying at the age of ninety-nine. The tomb has a Purbeck marble slab which is covered with brasses.

STOKE BRUERNE, close to Roade and just off the A508 is probably better known for its position on the Grand Union Canal and for its Canal Museum, but the church of **ST MARY** dates back to the Normans and part of the tower is still of that period. The two windows and pointed arch by the nave are Norman, and the upper part of the tower is Perpendicular, as are other sections of the church. The restored rood screen is medieval dating from around 1420 and either side of the altar in the south aisle are lanterns - perhaps this chapel was used by the canal visitors. The east window in the chancel dates from the fifteenth century and look for the original doorway to the rood loft in the north aisle and the tomb to the left.

PATTISHALL, situated on the A5 Watling Street is approximately four miles from Towcester and includes the villages of Astcote, Eastcote, Dalscote and Fosters Booth. The church is dedicated to the **HOLY CROSS**, and is situated on rising ground at the north east end of the village and consists of a nave and side aisles, south porch, chancel, and a low tower. The nave is part Saxon as can be seen from the north-west angle outside and the north east angle inside and the chancel arch and blocked north doorway are Norman. There are thirteenth century arcades and the tower was rebuilt in 1663 but the remainder of the church is of the Perpendicular era.

TIFFIELD church dedicated to **ST JOHN THE BAPTIST** consists of a small unbuttressed tower of the Decorated period, nave, north aisle, south porch and chancel. The church was restored in 1859 when the body of the church was rebuilt together with the south aisle and south porch and the rest of the church was restored in 1873. The octagonal font is Norman - look for the lovely leaf carvings around it. Also look to find a gable cross set into the south wall, this was discovered in the foundations during the rebuilding

TOWCESTER claims to be the oldest town in Northamptonshire. It is situated on the great Roman military road called Watling Street, now the A5. Historians speculate regarding the Roman garrison and its buildings, but the church of **ST LAWRENCE** has found considerable remains of a Roman flooring and tiles from a hypocaust. These were discovered in the south aisle and under the arch nearest to the chancel. On the south wall outside the church you can view part of the herring bone Roman floor discovered in 1983. The church was probably first built by the Saxons around AD920 and there are also traces of a Norman building. On the south side of the chancel arch there is a Norman zigzag shaft, which may also be sitting on a round Saxon stone. The shaft is dated around 1120 and was incorporated in the chancel arch in 1871. The remainder of the church is of the medieval period, although there has been restoration work throughout the years. William Sponne rector of Towcester from 1422 to 1448 and later became Archdeacon of Norfolk was a great benefactor to the town. He purchased Sponne House, then an inn in 1440, the grammar school was founded under his will and was originally housed in the Chantry Chapel near the church. The table tomb to Archdeacon Sponne lies to the south of the chancel in his own 'Chantry Chapel' and in the same chapel is the Sponne east window. The church, like the town, suffered during the Civil War when it was fortified by Prince Rupert. Towcester during the war was the only Royalist stronghold.

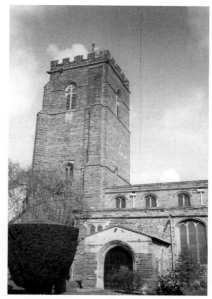

HULCOTE is the estate hamlet of the **EASTON NESTON** parish and included in this parish is Sewardsley for it was here there was a Priory of nuns of the Cistertion order founded by Richard de Lestre who was the lord of the manor in the reign of Henry II. Easton Neston is now the home of Lord Hesketh and the eighteenth century house is set in beautiful parkland on the outskirts of Towcester. The church of **ST MARY** situated in the grounds of the estate contains many memorials to the Fermors who first bought and owned the estate during the seventeenth century. There is a lovely table tomb memorial and brass on a slab of Purbeck marble. The Hesketh memorials do not begin until the first Lord Hesketh who died in 1944. In the eastern end of the north aisle and over the arch there is a wall painting. The painting is of walls, towers, turrets, gables, windows and kneeling angels - probably 'Heavenly Jerusalem' with angels among them. The description on the wall suggests that the paintings might have been part of an overall scheme, centering on the former subject in the stained glass window and which was possibly 'Our Lord in Glory'.

PAULERSPURY, a short drive along the A5 from Towcester and you arrive at the village where William Carey one of Northamptonshire's famous sons was born in 1761. William Carey was a Baptist minister who founded the Baptist Missionary Society and spent forty years of his life in India.
The church dedicated to **ST JAMES** recognises Carey's work with a memorial tablet situated in the church porch:

TO THE GLORY OF GOD
AND IN
MEMORY OF Wm CAREY
MISSIONARY AND ORIENTALIST
WHO WAS BORN AT PAULERSPURY AUGUST 17 1961
DIED AT SERAMPORE, INDIA
JUNE 9TH 1834

Also to the right of the porch is his father's grave. Edmund his father taught at the village school.
St James' Church has a thirteenth century chancel and a Perpendicular tower but the body of the church was rebuilt in 1843-44. Look for the round Norman font, showing

that there probably was a church here then, and also the superb double piscina and triple sedilia from the fourteenth century which has a rich carving of a canopy of leaves and a frieze of ivy leaves with snakes and dragons.

Just off the A508 from Grafton Regis we find the village of **ALDERTON** and the church of **ST MARGARET**. Although the church was built during the fourteenth century, the tower was built earlier and restored during the sixteenth century. The church was largely rebuilt during the nineteenth century and retaining for instance the font, beautifully carved pulpit and monuments from earlier periods. Before the Reformation the church was also famous for its paintings of the saints. On the floor in the chancel is an old wooden figure thought to represent Sir William Combemartyn who died in 1318. This is a rare monument as it is thought that less than one hundred of these have survived from the medieval period.

GRAFTON REGIS is a small village steeped in history and Royal connections - indeed Edward IV married Elizabeth Woodville, her family owning the manor and later both Richard III and Henry VIII stayed in Grafton. The church of **ST MARY**, built mainly during the twelfth to fourteenth centuries offers marvellous peaceful views looking over the valley and canal. There are still several examples of the early building despite repairs and extensions over the years. The north arcading, the sedilia and piscina are all early examples as is the tub-shaped Norman font. A medieval panel from an old screen shows the betrayal of Christ and there are a variety of memorials to the Woodville's and Fitroy's. The altar tomb of freestone with an alabaster top in memory of John Woodville (1415) is worth seeing.

POTTERSPURY village is a few miles from Stony Stratford and on the A5 Watling Street, with a church dating back to 1087. Lying close to Whittlebury forest the village had associations with the Duke of Grafton who built Wakefield Lodge close by during the eighteenth century. Interestingly the third Duke of Grafton, Augustus Fitzroy was Prime Minister in 1767! **ST NICHOLAS'** Church was built during thirteenth and fourteenth centuries and, although it has been greatly restored during the nineteenth century still retains Norman carvings on the capitals of the pillars in the north arcade, and its font. The church has some box pews, possibly for the Lords of the Manor and there is a brass memorial to a forest ranger who died in 1633. The Dukes of Grafton were hereditary rangers of the forest.

COSGROVE, situated close to the Buckingham border and the A5 is the point at which the Grand Union Canal enters the county. The church of **ST PETER AND ST PAUL** had extensive restoration during the eighteenth century but is still nearly a thousand years old. The chancel dates from about 1180 and outside on the eastern end are the remains of a typical Anglo-Norman triple window and arcading. Also outside on the north wall are the pillars and arch of a late thirteenth century doorway. Although the chancel arch was damaged by fire in 1586 it is still possible to see a late medieval wall painting on the wall above

the arch. The imposing tower was built during the fourteenth century and the weathercock is reputed to be early
eighteenth century. The fifteenth century roof with its oak
timbers is worth seeing - it was discovered in the 1930's
when the old eighteenth century plaster was removed.

The deserted village of **FURTHO** used to be on the main
London to Northampton road, but now it lies just off the
A508 between Cosgrove and Stony Stratford and consists
of a church, medieval dovecote and a farm house. **ST
BARTHOLOMEW'S** was rebuilt in 1620, restored in
1870 and then, after the last service in 1921, left to decay.
Now under the guidance of 'The Churches Conservation
Trust' the church has been renovated and the surrounding
area tidied to present a picturesque and quiet spot. The
church was originally built during the early seventeenth
century and much of the furniture removed to other
churches after it ceased to be used. Since its renovation an
altar has been brought in and according to a local parish-
ioner one service a year is held - possibly on St
Bartholomew's Day.

The Redundant Church at St Peter and St Paul, Preston Deanery (page 20)

Brackley & The South West

The open rural countryside between Daventry and Brackley enables the traveller to explore a feast of superbly picturesque scenery, with often small hamlets nestling together around a ridge or stream. The Northamptonshire Heights extending south towards Brackley provide the source for several rivers - the Nene, Tove and Ouse.

In this quiet and peaceful rural area of the county, with many unspoilt villages often mentioned in the Domesday Book, the traveller will be delighted with the opportunities available to explore the counties historic past. Often the only noise to shatter the peace will come from the international racing circuit at Silverstone.

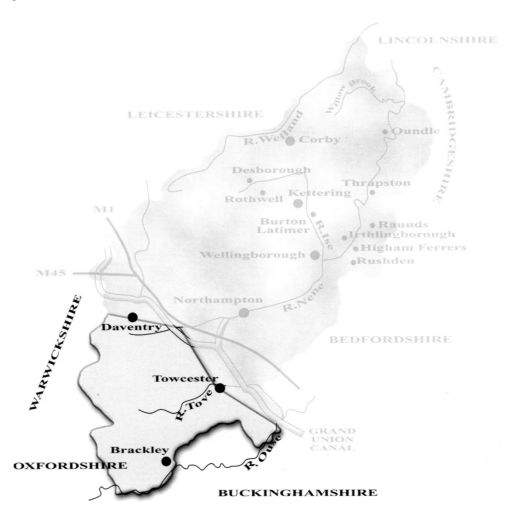

VERDON village situated in beautiful countryside on the Northamptonshire Heights has woods close by that attract visitors each year for their display of bluebells. The poet Thomas Gray frequently stayed with his uncle, William Antrobus who was vicar at Everdon between 1729 and 1744, and it is thought that whilst on one of his visits the churchyard was his inspiration for his 'Elegy'. **ST MARY'S CHURCH**, an enormous building in comparison to the small village, is mainly of the fourteenth century, although there is a Norman font and a large collection of medieval faces and queer creatures looking out from the tower and windows, and inside wooden carved comic heads of the original roof. It is thought that prosperous local people together with the monks of Bernay in Normandy combined to create the large church. At the time of the Domesday Book (1066) much of Everdon was owned by the Benedictine Abbey of Bernay. The church has been restored over the centuries but admire the east window in the south aisle, find the painted coat of arms of Thomas Spencer and his wife and the pelican in the north window of the nave.

ST MARY'S standing in the middle of **FARTHINGSTONE** village, called in Domesday time Farraxton, is built of local stone. The Norman church was restored during the mid-nineteenth century. Inside the church look for the lovely poppyhead bench ends to find amongst others a monkey with cymbals, a devil with a kitten and a donkey. Also have a good look at the lovely stained glass, one window is in memory of Enid Jocelyn Joy who died in 1921 aged 22 years, she was daughter of Philip Agnew who moved into the village in the early twentieth century and was looked upon as the 'squire'. He became High Sheriff of Northampton, but sadly also lost his only son in the First World War. There is a garden of remembrance in the village called 'Joymead', which is open to the public and each year around 13 July the Joymead Tea is held in memory of Joy Agnew.

Also look for the lovely sundial on the church wall as you walk up the church yard, the letters in latin translate, "At this very moment, eternity is at hand."

There is some interesting history regarding the replacement of the church clock. It was replaced in 1894 and installed by John Smith and sons from Derby. The church archives shows a hand written estimate in copper-plate and on heavy parchment, and it goes on to describe all the work needed. It states, "The entire cost of the clock complete and fixed and inclusive of all carriage and travelling expenses, clock makers time during fixing but exclusively of any woodwork or masons work required during fixing would be £65"!

On a hill to the north of the village is is Castle Dykes, the earthwork of a medieval castle.

ST MARY'S CHURCH, FAWSLEY stands isolated in Fawsley Park, but once part of the now deserted medieval village of Fawsley. Evidence suggests that the church was built during the thirteenth century and added to and altered over the centuries. It

has also been suggested that a wooden Saxon church may have been on the site earlier.

The church is a rich mausoleum to the Knightleys who owned the hall for around four centuries, since the reign of Henry VI. There are many memorials including brasses to Thomas Knightley (1516) and his wife Joan, and to Sir Edward Knightley (1542) and Maude his wife (1557). On the south side of the nave are the recumbent alabaster effigies of Sir Richard Knightley (1534) and Joan his wife. There are beautifully carved medieval box pews and and some old glass with scenes including the Good Samaritan, Last Supper and the Crucifixion. An

interesting feature is the Knightley box pew in the south aisle. This high-sided pew enabled the Knightley family to be hidden from the rest of the congregation but a squint in the south wall of the chancel enabled them to see the priest. Explore the church and you will find a wealth of interest to a fascinating family who had a large influence on local history.

WEEDON village is on the main A5 Watling Street and the church is severed from the village by the railway viaduct and is surrounded on the other side by the raised bank of the Grand Union Canal. So it's under the viaduct and into the well maintained churchyard to see the goose weathervane sitting on the top of the Norman west tower.

Above: The magnificent Knightley, Fawlsey.

The Church is dedicated to **ST PETER AND ST PAUL** and to the south of this site there once stood a chapel dedicated to St Werburgh and also possibly a priory. St Werburgh is best know for banishing a flock of wild geese which were plaguing the local cornfields. The geese obeyed her, vanished and have never been seen since. Hence the weathervane! The body of the church was largely rebuilt during the nineteenth century although the tower stands on its Norman foundations and there is a fifteenth century doorway.

Search the churchyard for the tomb of a lady Alice Old. Described by Arthur Mee in

1946 as, *"a lady who lived in the reign of six sovereigns, born during the reign of Elizabeth, and dying during the reign of William & Mary. She would hear of Drake and Raleigh and would hear the bells tolling for Queen Elizabeth I. She may have seen the Gunpowder Plot and men fleeing for their lives towards Ashby St Ledgers, and perhaps some survivors from Naseby came limping through the village"*. Mee continues to say that she may have heard tales of the Great Plague and Great Fire of London and even seen the 'glow in the sky' when Northampton was burned down. What a momentous period of history for Alice.

Two small villages, **CHURCH STOWE** and **LITTLE STOWE** combine to make the parish of **STOWE NINE CHURCHES** and there are several stories associated with the strange name. Is it possible to see nine churches from the high ground; has the name itself been adapted; was the lord of the manor patron to nine churches, or is it true that the fairies objecting to the building on their 'Fairy Ring' knocked the initial building down eight times before a praying monk helped the builders succeed at the ninth attempt? All very strange, interesting and will probably remain unsolved for ever!

The church, dedicated to **ST MICHAEL** has a rare Saxon tower with a medieval (Perpendicular), top and there is a Norman north doorway. The rest of the church is mainly late Perpendicular with the chancel being built around 1860. Several monuments within the church are worth exploring, one of Sir Gerald de L'Isle 1287 in well preserved marble and the other carved ten years before her death in 1630 of Lady Danvers - both are masterpieces in their own right.

COLD HIGHAM so called from its exposed and elevated position. One tale we were told is that there is nothing in the way to stop the icy cold winds of the Russian Steppes sweeping their way into the village!

The small church dedicated to **ST LUKE** was built during the great building age with Norman work in the nave, a thirteenth century saddleback roof and a splendid fourteenth century oak carving of a cross-legged knight wearing plate armour. He was Sir John de Patteshull, Lord of the Manor who died in 1350 and he lies in the side chapel on the south side of the church. Look on the right side of the choir stalls and you will see a leper's squint. This is a small window where the lepers can sit away from the congregation and watch the priest through the window during services.

It is thought that a Saxon church stood on the site where the chancel now is, but there was certainly a large church in **LITCHBOROUGH** in Norman times as the thickness of the walls indicate, together with the round font and the piers of the nave arcades. **ST MARTIN'S CHURCH,** seems to have had additional building during the next three centuries, with iron and woodwork of the doors being part of the original building. Look for the three human carved heads above the entrance to the north porch and the tomb to Sir John Needham 1618, dressed as a knight in armour with his legs crossed. The three heads show joy, horror and the third one has a demon with its fingers in the eyes of the head. Also find the unusual window containing a sundial which is reported to be over two hundred years old. This shows the sun as a smiling head with the hours marked around a kind of scallop.

BLAKESLEY. The church dedicated to the **VIRGIN MARY** was largely built of ironstone during the medieval period and has a tower, aisles, chancel, clerestory windows and a scratch dial of that period. Perhaps the most interesting monument in the church is a brass portrait mounted on the wall. Dressed in armour and hands in prayer with a lion at his feet Matthew Swetenham was bow-bearer to Henry IV! On his memorial there is a Latin inscription which when translated reads:

"Here lies Matthew Swetenham formerly bearer of the bow and esquire of the most illustrious King Henry the Fourth who died on the 29th. day of the month of December in the year of our Lord 1416 to whose soul may God be merciful. Amen."

The historian Baker could not trace any connection which Swetenham had with Blakesley, but he had a lease of the manor of Weedon Pinkney from Anne the Queen of King Richard II. He was Sheriff of the county in the fourteenth year of King Henry IV. Look for the corbels along the nave with faces at the base of the arches and the table tomb of Roger Wake, who was sheriff of the county in 1483..

The **HOLY CROSS CHURCH, BYFIELD** was built in 1242 of rich Northamptonshire stone has a fine lofty tower, added to over the years to show five stages and rising to a massive 140 feet. Explore the church and find the three seater sedilia, the beautifully carved bench ends, the gargoyles in the porch and the interesting note if you took sanctuary in the church.

If you took sanctuary in the church you could not be forcibly removed for forty days, during that time you had to take an oath of abjuration before a coroner and proceed to a seaport nominated by him. After forty days you went on your way penniless clothed in a sackcloth and carrying a white

wooden cross, you then proceeded to the port directed by the coroner not spending more than one night in any place and not to waiver off the Queens/Kings highway. On reaching the port, if there is no vessel for him he must, daily walk into the sea up to his waist. If in forty days there is no ship then he must go into the church and start again.

Two villages **UPPER AND LOWER BODDINGTON** have one church dedicated to **ST JOHN THE BAPTIST.** The church was built during the fifteenth century, although there are earlier dated tombs found in the church. Its main treasure is an unusual old chest, about six feet long and carved out of a solid log of oak. William Proctor, a rector who died in 1627 has his portrait in brass.

PRESTON CAPES offers a lovely panoramic view of the county including two iron age camps - Arbury Hill and Borough Hill, together with the Nene Valley.
The church dedicated to **ST PETER AND ST PAUL** is entered through the lovely wrought iron gateway into the churchyard. It has a Perpendicular tower surmounted by battlements. It is suggested that the oldest part of the church is the nave arcade, the round south pillars were built around 1200 and the north pillars about a hundred years later. The great iron studded door is approximately four hundred years old. Note as you enter the porch the Holy Water Stoup, (water basin). The church was drastically restored in 1853. We stood in wonder at the beautifully engraved glass east window, installed in 1974, and engraved by Annabel Rathbone in memory of George St John Ravenshear, who died in 1972 at the age of ten - his face appears as that of St. George. The window was given by his relations and friends, including Lord St John of Fawsley. Look in the chancel for the grotesque corbels. These are reputed to be Saxon fertility corbels which seem to have been reset on the chancel walls. There are also beautiful medieval choir stalls with richly carved ornamental bench ends. In the churchyard on the eastern side of the church porch is the base of an ancient preaching cross. This was used for worship before the church was built. Look for the head of the cross set into the outside of the east wall of the south aisle and behind the window.

HELLIDON village is one of the highest villages in the county and lies adjacent to the Warwickshire border and uniquely three rivers the Leam, Cherwell and Nene all rise in the village or close by.
The church of **ST JOHN THE BAPTIST** is affectionately known to most people in Northamptonshire as the "Honey Church" due to the fact that after the Second World War and when the bells had been silent the bees had made over one hundredweight of honey in the clock works! The church claims to have been built in 1591 as the date on the lintel over the south door shows but the tower was built around 1350, so although there have been additions and restorations the church is much older than would appear.
As you enter the church notice the deep grooves in the stonework either side of the doorway. The story is that these grooves were made by the soldiers sharpening their swords before the Battle of Edgehill in 1642.
Inside the door on the south wall is the wonderful memorial window to the fallen of the First World War (the village never had a fatality in the Second World War). The window which may be unique depicts the faces of the four men who lost their lives, together with St George and St Michael.

MAIDFORD, known in Domesday times as Merdeford is a charming village situated on a small tributary to the River Tove and close to Preston Capes. The thirteenth century church of **ST PETER AND ST PAUL**, next page, has a tower from that period which has a rare saddleback roof. The village is traditionally known for its lacemaking and for many years during the nineteenth century had a thriving industry - Leopold

Stanton in the 1850's even based the design of his driveway gate on a Maltese lace pattern and the gate became known as 'The Old Lace Gate'! Appropriately lace work is interwoven into the church altar cloths.

ST MARY'S CHURCH, WOODFORD-HALSE is built of sandstone, has stood here for over 700 years and was restored in 1878. We enter the church through a thirteenth century doorway and there is some fine examples of Perpendicular and Early English architecture in the chancel and north arcade, with one capital of the late Norman period. There are some lovely old fifteenth century bench ends worked in with the modern seating and the font dates from around 1660. Look around for a brass figure of a priest, a former vicar, Nicholas Stafford (1400). In the chancel is a stone effigy of a female figure one Maud Holland (1330) which was discovered on the north side during the extensive restoration in 1878.

The delightful fourteenth century church of **ALL SAINTS**, situated within the village of **ADSTONE** on the old Banbury Lane, was totally restored during the nineteenth century when the chancel was also added.
In Catholic times it was served by the Canons of Ashby, and no provision having been made for it after the Reformation. The curate was supported by subscriptions of the lord of the manor and the principal inhabitants.

Sitting on the Banbury Lane the small village of **CANONS ASHBY** with its church dedicated to **ST MARY** is all that is left of the priory of Augustinian Canons founded in Henry II's time over eight hundred years ago. Sadly the cloisters and monastic buildings have all been destroyed. The church is the west end of the priory church and was therefore much larger during its time of the Augustinian Canons. What remains of the monastic church is the nave with the north aisle, the tower being added during the fourteenth century and the Decorated period. The west doorway and the arcade on each side were probably added during the middle of the thirteenth century.

Canons Ashby house, now managed by the National Trust was built during the sixteenth century and became the home of the Dryden family and was frequented by John Dryden who became the Poet Laureate in 1670. The church has several memorials to the Dryden family.

Two photographs of Culworth Corbels

CULWORTH, famous for the Culworth Gang. A band of robbers who terrorised the area for twenty years during the late eighteenth century, and for Charles I who stayed here prior to his battle nearby at Cropredy Bridge. **ST MARY'S CHURCH**, next page, has had a lot of restoration during the nineteenth century but was originally built during the thirteenth and fourteenth centuries. There is still a beautifully carved Jacobean pulpit and the original bench ends. Before leaving note the tombstone to the right of the church entrance, it is the grave of a young black servant boy.

Close to the church is a mound said to be the site of a castle built by the manorial barons and built during King Stephen's reign.

SULGRAVE, in our opinion must rank as the second most historical village in the county after Fotheringhay, for it can probably boast to be the home of democracy in the United States of America. It was in this village and the manor house that Lawrence Washington who built in 1560. The house remained with the Washington family until 1656 and soon after this date it was sold. First mentioned at the time of the Domesday survey of 1086 and later belonging to the Priory of St Andrew Northampton it went to the crown in 1539 and was sold to Lawrence Washington. In 1656 Colonel John Washington left these shores to live in Virginia. He was the great grandfather of George Washington the first President of the United States of America. In 1914 Sulgrave Manor was given by British subscribers to the people of Great Britain and the United States of America, in celebration of the hundred years of peace between the two nations.

ST JAMES THE LESS, although built during the reign of Edward III (1327-1377) has Saxon origins and perhaps the original building was in another part of the village. The west door is typical of Saxon construction. The church has several links with the Washington family. Above the entrance to the south porch is the date 1564, which was the year in which Lawrence Washington's wife Amee died. Was the porch built in her memory? In the south aisle in front of the medieval piscina stands the Washington Pew and in the window above are the Coats of Arms of three generations of the Washington family. In front of the pew Lawrence Washington, his wife and their eldest son, Robert are buried.

HERE LIETH THE BODE OF LAVRENCE WASHINGTON SONNE AND HEIRE OF ROBERT WASHINGTON OF SOVLGRAVE IN THE COVNTIE OF NORTHAMPTON ESQUIER WHO MARRIED MARGARET THE ELDEST DAUGHTER OF WILLIAM BUTLER OF TEES IN THE COUNTIE OF SUSSEX ESQUIER WHO HAD ISSU BY HER 8 SONS AND 9 DAUGHTERS WHICH LAVRENCE DECEASED THE 13 OF DEC. A.D. DNI 1616

Of special interest and hanging on the wall by the pew is a colourful chart tracing back the Washington family tree through the Earl of Lancaster and Henry III to King John and Magna Carta. According to local tradition the original large oak chest belonged to the Washington family. Several other gifts from American pilgrims enrich the church, the light oak screen and the organ being just two. Finally before leaving the church, children will be amused with the hand-drawn hearse - not many of these about now.

MORETON PINKNEY lies close to Canons Ashby and the old Banbury Lane with the church of **ST MARY** being built in the thirteenth century and the beautiful chancel rebuilt in 1845 and the same plan used by Cardinal Newman at Littlemore. There is a round Norman font and the Early English arcades are supported by Norman pillars and also look for the Norman scratch dial in the wall.

The story read from the history sheet in the church tells of the near destruction of the church in 1893. It seems that in the winter of that year they had the stove alight to warm the church and the very hot chimney pipe set alight the woodwork in the tower. When the fire was discovered a lad was sent on a pony to Banbury to get the fire brigade. After a difficult journey over frost bound roads the fire brigade and the villagers efforts saved the body of the church but the tower was completely destroyed. Most of the bells had to be re-cast, and the clock was replaced in memory of the Bishop Oxenden of Montreal, who was a frequent visitor to Moreton Pinkney. It seems hard to imagine a journey on horseback to raise the fire brigade.

THORPE MANDEVILLE has strong connections with Oliver Cromwell who was garrisoned in the manor house during the Civil War. The manor house, now destroyed, was owned by the Kirtons who were related to Cromwell. The

church of **ST JOHN THE BAPTIST** has a monument to Thomas Kirton, 1601 and his wife, 1597, kneeling on either side of a table with their twelve children. Explore further monuments, including one to Henry Pullen, rector who was also chaplain to the Artic expedition of 1875 and lead by Sir Robert Nares. The church is mainly of the Decorated period with a rare recessed saddleback roof. Look for the small figure high up on the outside of the tower, is this John the Baptist? The church was restored during the second half of the nineteenth century and one of these dates 1887 is set into the fabric of the church, together with the initials of the rector at the time.

WAPPENHAM, a small village situated between Towcester and Brackley and the church of **ST MARY** has brasses commemorating the Lovatt family of Astwell Manor. Full figure brasses and the family coat of arms are embedded in the floor in front of the south aisle altar and came from Biddlesden Abbey after the dissolution of the monasteries in the reign of Henry VIII. In front of the chancel steps there is a brass of a knight in armour, and in the centre of the aisle there is a large brass commemorating Sir Thomas Billing. To help preserve the brass it is covered with a rug. The church, dating from the thirteenth century, has a fine pinnacle tower and a wide chancel and this may have been connected with the foundation of an uncommonly large chantry in the church in 1327 for the warden and five priests. Look for the 'squint' or hagioscope in the aisle, now blocked up but it enabled the priest at the chantry to see what was happening in the chancel.

WEEDON LOIS church dedicated to **ST MARY** is one of our cruciform churches, that is to say the tower or steeple is in the centre. The church is partly Early English the central tower is embattled and there is Norman evidence in the form of some herring bone masonry in the west wall and the tower. The chapel is separated from the aisle by a carved screen and the circular font is Norman. Look for the wall paintings over the east arch in the south aisle. The pulpit is stone and dates from 1849, it has an unusual doorway into the pulpit and there is some lovely carved stone work above the doorway. You go through two arches to reach the altar. Look around

the ends of the arches to find many head-corbels. In the churchyard extension is a memorial to Dame Edith Sitwell and designed by Henry Moore. This unique memorial is in the shape of a tapering slab and a bronze plaque with two hands, signifying Youth and Age.

An attractive story is told of William Losse who was vicar at the time of the Civil War and when the Roundheads came to arrest him during a service he barricaded himself into the central tower. They wounded him through the trap door and seeing blood drip down left him for dead, but he survived and there is a brass in the church recounting this incident.

ST BOTOLPH'S CHURCH, SLAPTON lies in picturesque surroundings on a hill above the River Tove. The church is small and was built over a relatively short period of time, starting with the Normans and being completed in the Early English period. The chancel is one of the smallest that we have seen, but it is the medieval paintings which, in their heyday must have greeted the worshipper with a blaze of colour. The paintings are all beautiful and realistic, but it is St Christopher on the north wall which is the most striking. The large painting of the Patron Saint of Travel, also has, in the bottom left corner, a mermaid. There are several other paintings including one of St George and the dragon and a rare one of St Eloi, the Patron Saint of Blacksmiths.

GREENS NORTON is named after the family of Greens, the ancient lords of the manor, the last one, the grandfather of Catherine Parr (Henry VIII's last wife) dying in 1506.

ST BARTHOLOMEW'S CHURCH with its slender spire was rebuilt in 1807 and 1957 but a church stood on the sight as early as the ninth century as is evidence from the Saxon window in the eastern wall of the nave. The circular font is Norman and is carved with flowers. Although there are still some fifteenth century monuments to the Greene family many were removed through wanton destruction during the eighteenth and nineteenth centuries.

Note the brass plates on a tomb in the north aisle let into the wall under an arch. On the floor in front of this tomb is a poor knight laying there with his lady and you cannot tell if he went on the crusades as his legs are missing below his knees. If a knight went on the crusades his legs were crossed. There is a carved screen across the centre aisle. As you pass the screen into the altar stalls, look up on the left and see a lovely carved memorial, the family are kneeling at prayer; they are William Hickey (1600) and his wife Francis (1603).

Spend some time wandering around this unusual church for few churches have evidence of a Saxon building. The church is unique in that within the building you have a fourteenth century medieval church, a Saxon tower, with a Renaissance belfry and modern spire. Also find the coat of arms of Elizabeth I by the belfry door. This is thought to be a rare sight as Cromwell's armies often destroyed such things. The Chantry House opposite the church would have been the home of the priests.

ABTHORPE, was originally a chapelry, in the Parish of Towcester; but was constituted a distinct parish, with the hamlets of Charlock and Foxcote in 1736 and sits on the banks of River Sow which changes it's name to the Tove on reaching Towcester.

ST JOHN THE BAPTIST CHURCH is sited on a slight mound in the centre of the village and is not very old by church architectural standards, for it was rebuilt in 1871 by money contributed by the Duke of Grafton. The Graftons had strong links with the village, owning much of the land until the 1920's, and the Grafton Hunt would meet on the village green. The church is unusual in that the tower with it's spire is at the north end of the church, as it possibly seems they did not have enough room at the west end, so they tucked the tower around the side.

BRADDEN'S church is dedicated to **ST MICHAEL** was rebuilt in 1850 with the exception of the tower and part of the nave arcades. An unusual statistic associated with the church is that the Rev Cornelious Ives who died in 1885 had been vicar for sixty five years. Quite a feat - the pulpit is in his memory.

WHITTLEBURY stands on the A413 Towcester to Buckingham road and has been the site of much Iron Age and Roman activity here and around the forest. Interestingly a local villager found a Roman skeleton in a shallow grave in his garden in 1983 and the vicar, because this had previously been a Christian burial reburied the skeleton in the churchyard. **ST MARY'S CHURCH**, and tower are mainly Early English architecture (1200-1300) although there is a Norman window high up in the tower and one capital on the north side is Norman. The church was restored during the late nineteenth century.

WICKEN was originally two parishes, Wyke Dyve and Wyke Hamoy and they were segregated by a brook running between them and acting as a parish boundary. They had two churches; St John's in Wyke Dyve and St James' in Wyke Hamon but in 1587 the parishes were reunited and **ST JOHN'S** church was completely rebuilt on a new site in 1770, except for the tower, and it replaced the old wooden thatched roof church.

The stained glass window of St George, King David and St Columba is in memory of the three sons of the famous family, Douglas-Pennant who were killed in the First World War.

Look for the magnificent brass across the whole floor of the chancel of George Sholto Gordon Douglas-Pennant who died in 1907. Look for other brasses in memory of local people, including the lovely one by the choir stalls and also do not miss the superb vaulted roof. There is also an old medieval wooden cross, right, in the churchyard.

WHITFIELD is another village on the A43 Brackley to Towcester road, with the Early English church dedicated to **ST JOHN THE EVANGE-**

LIST. The church is now fairly new and had to be rebuilt after the tower and spire came down in a gale on 7 February 1869 and totally wrecking the church fabric. Fairly modern stained glass dated 1898-1914.

SYRESHAM situated just off the A43 Towcester to Brackley road. **ST JAMES' CHURCH**, although having a Norman font, south doorway, north window and dogtooth chancel arch, has also been heavily restored on several occasions, the latest in 1874. The church was mainly built during the twelfth and thirteenth centuries but thankfully, even though some of its charm has been lost due to restoration several aspects of Norman architecture remain. Syresham has an unusual record of having a martyr. He is John Kurde, a shoemaker who was burnt at the stake for his religious beliefs in 1557 in Northampton. The memorial in the Wesleyan Chapel, Syresham reads:

'In memory of John Kurde, shoemaker, the Syresham martyr, burnt at the stake in defence of the truth, 1557. Tell ye your children of it, and let your children tell their children, and their children another generation.'

From Brackley we follow the A422 towards Middleton Cheney and just after Farthinghoe find a turning on your right leading to the small village of **THENFORD**. The church of **ST MARY** lies isolated in a field with a farm nearby. Evidence suggests that the Romans were active in the area but the church may have been built during the late Norman/Early Perpendicular period. There is a Norman font and the south doorway's rounded arch, south aisle, west and east windows together with the south arcade suggest a period of around 1200. There is a lovely old stained glass window in which St Peter is walking on the waves supporting a fish under his feet. Find the ancient poor box by the south door and the monument with the effigy of Fulk Woodhull who died in 1613, he is the ancestor of Michael Woodhull a well known collector of books, whose library was dispersed in the early 1900's.

WARKWORTH church like so many others stands isolated in a field, is dedicated to **ST MARY** and was heavily restored and rebuilt in 1840-1. It is well known for its magnificent tombs to the Lyons and Chetwode families. They owned Warkworth Castle which was demolished in 1805. The table top tomb of Sir John Lyons in the north aisle, is possibly the best example of a mid-fourteenth tomb of its kind in the country. The tomb which is high and narrow is made of very hard chalk, is enriched with figures and shields and is a good example of the military period costume (1350). Look for other monuments to the Lyons and Chetwolds around the church.

PLUMPTON, a small village a few miles west of Towcester with the church of **ST JOHN THE BAPTIST** rebuilt in 1822 but with the tower, arch, chancel, font and box pews from an earlier age. There is a monument to an Anna Moore who died in 1683.

RADSTONE is reached off the A43 from Helmdon and has only a few houses with the church tucked away up a little green lane opposite the old school house. Dedicated to **ST LAURENCE**, shown left, the church is unusual in that the lovely tower has a Norman basement (c.1150), with the middle stage Early English (c.1250), and the top a saddleback roof of the Decorated period (c.1370). The nave and the aisle are also Decorated and the font is Norman.

SILVERSTONE, famous throughout the world for the British Grand Prix of motor racing and other motor sports, but the village situated on the A43 between Towcester and Brackley recalls its origins at the heart of Whittlebury Forest where inhabitants made their living from charcoal burning and other woodland crafts. During the twelfth century King John had a hunting lodge here and Luffield Abbey lay on the Buckinghamshire border. The small eighteenth century church of **ST MICHAEL** was rebuilt in 1884.

KINGS SUTTON church is dedicated to **ST PETER AND ST PAUL** and has in our opinion the most graceful and finest spire in the county if not the country. It dominates the countryside for miles around rising to a height of 198 feet, and with it's delicate pinnacles, flying buttresses and a tower with windows to allow the light through is truly an astounding sight. It is likely that there has been a church on this site for well over a thousand years and perhaps even associated with the youngest saint, Rumwold, the youngest son of the King of Northumbria who only lived for three days in 662AD. The chancel is Norman with remarkable Norman arcading on the inner walls and

Norman piers and carvings in the nave. The six-sided font is Norman and seems to have been crudely hewn from the stone, unlike the capitals on the piers which have better carvings. Over the years the church building, mainly of the Decorated period has been added to and restored but with the spire remaining its most remarkable feature. A local story suggests that when the spire was built it was done so in competition with two others - Bloxham and Adderbury in Oxfordshire but when the judge was asked for an opinion he came up with the following: *'Bloxham for length, Adderbury for strength, King's Sutton for beauty'*!

In the hamlet of Astrop, close to King's Sutton, there is a spring known as St Rumwold and this made Kings Sutton a fashionable health resort during the seventeenth century. All that is left now, is a well in the park.

MARSTON ST LAWRENCE, village lies in rolling countryside between Banbury and Brackley and has a church dedicated to **ST LAWRENCE**, the size and vastness creating immediate impact upon entering inside. The church dates from the eleventh century but much of the building is of the Perpendicular and Decorated period of architecture. There is a beautifully carved dark oak Jacobean screen in the tower arch and dated around 1610. Look for the three sedilia seats which look extremely odd being very close to the floor. This was due entirely to the floor being raised and retiled in the nineteenth century. There are memorials to the Blencowe family who received the estate from Henry VI and were lords of the manor for more than five centuries until the estate was sold soon after the First World War. Sir John Blencowe, born in the village in 1642, whose monument is in church was Baron of the Exchequer and died in 1726. As you leave the church admire the magnificent yew tree which is over one thousand years old.

EYDON, a beautiful picturesque village situated in the south of the county and close to the Cotswolds, and with its stocks still on the green dates form the Domesday period.

Much of **ST NICHOLAS' CHURCH** has been restored during 1864-65 but there is still a superb Norman font and work from the earlier architectural periods. There has probably been a church in Eydon since the mid-twelfth century and the squat tower is fourteenth century, as is the battered effigy of a lady in the vestry. The Norman pillars in the north arcade support the fourteenth century arches. The lady in the vestry is reputed to be that of the wife of Sir Richard Wale, Lord of the Manor in Edward II's reign.

MIDDLETON CHENEY is a large village lying on the main Banbury to Brackley road and the church dedicated to **ALL SAINTS** is one of the best Decorated period churches in the county and was built by the rector William of Edyngton. William later became Bishop of Winchester and built the west door of the cathedral. The church was heavily restored in 1865 by Sir Gilbert Scott.

The lofty and embattled tower, with the unusual number of eight pinnacles, carrying a tall and graceful spire is Perpendicular. The porch is unusual as it is built with interlocking stones and has no timber. The church is perhaps also known for its stained glass windows and the west window has six small lights depicting the Six Days of Creation, (the seventh being the Sabbath and the day of rest). Interestingly, during the Civil War there was a Battle of Middleton in 1643, during which over two hundred Roundheads were killed and many are buried in the churchyard.

GREATWORTH stands on a hill and is just south of the old drove road, Welsh Lane, used for taking stock from Wales to London. The small church of **ST PETER** was built mainly between the thirteenth and fifteenth centuries, the oldest part being the base of the north arch leading from the nave to the tower, although it is quite possible that a Saxon church was built earlier on the site. As with many churches restoration, rebuilding and additions have taken place over the centuries, with major rebuilding during the late nineteenth century. There is a brass in the church indicating the American Washington connection. The Pargiter family lived here from the reign of Henry VIII and subsequently acquired the manor and it was the daughter of Robert Pargiter, Amy, who married Laurence Washington of Sulgrave and there was also a Dorothy Pargiter who married Sir John Washington and you find him at Thrapston, the younger brother of Laurence.

HELMDON, near Brackley has a church dedicated to **ST MARY MAGDALENE** and was largely built during the thirteenth and fourteenth centuries, although there was a Saxon stone church earlier and has continued with much restoration and additional building work. The earliest item in the church is the Early English piscina near the north door, but also look in the chancel and find the sedilia with serious and comical carvings, below right. The magnificent yew in the churchyard is reputed to be about 2000 years old. The church is worth a visiting to admire the yew. The lovely east window represents the birth, death, and resurrection of Jesus Christ.

From Brackley take the country lanes to **HINTON IN THE HEDGES** to be greeted by a lovely serene and quiet village with the green as the village focal point. Originally Hinton lay on the main eighteenth century turnpike road between Banbury and Buckingham and the village is named after Sir William Hinton who held this manor in 1346.
The church dedicated to the **HOLY TRINITY**, has a Norman tower and font but most of the fabric of the church is Early English. Traces of Saxon masonry have been found suggesting that there may have been an earlier church on this site. Look for the unusual tomb of Sir William Hinton who is laying, not side by side as you would expect with Lady Hinton, but with his wife laying at his feet in a straight line! Interestingly, Sir William dressed as a medieval knight, is one of only a few in the country of this period, dressed in a short sleeved surcoat and armed with a rare dagger.

FARTHINGHOE'S church dedicated to **St Michael** has a large Norman tower, thirteenth century arcade with carvings on some of the capitals, and a fifteenth century clerestory. An interesting and unusual feature is the one handed tower clock under which is the date 1654, being the year in which a Sir

Above: Farthinghowe grave marker

John Egerton repaired the tower. There is a fine carved marble statue just as you enter the church and it is of George Rush who died in London in 1803, and it shows him reading a book in a thoughtful mood dressed in a loose gown and wearing slippers. He is thought to have been lord of the manor. On the left as you reach the choir stalls you will see a doorway which was the stairs leading up to the rood screen which stretched across the aisle and separated the choir from the congregation.

EDGECOTE lies six miles from Banbury and has a few scattered houses and the manor and church. The manor was rebuilt in the eighteenth century for Richard Chauncey and it replaced an earlier one that Charles I and his two sons are reputed to have rested on the night of the 22 October 1642, prior to the Battle of Edgehill.

Close to the manor house is the church dedicated to **ST JAMES**. It sits in the park close to the manor house. It consists of a nave, south aisle and porch, north chapel and chancel. The interior is well paved and pewed. There is neither an arch or division between the nave and chancel; on the south side within the altar rails is a piscina and a plain locker and the east window of stained glass was a gift by Thomas Carter. See if you can find on the arcade that separates the nave from the aisle a carved skull and hand on one of the capitals, they are possibly Early English.

The treasures of this church are its monuments to the Chauncey family. They were Lords of the Manor for three centuries. Sir William Chauncey and Joan his wife lie in alabaster on Elizabethan tombs. Sir Toby who died in 1607 lies between his two wives - it is said that the figures around the tomb are those of their children. They are beautiful tombs elaborately carved.

The Cartwright family, Lords of the Manor at Aynho are in the windows, and look around for the brass tablet of Arden Bayly who was minister here for 49 years during the nineteenth century. The church leaflet tells us interestingly that the north chapel, now the vestry, was once arranged with two floors, and the priest lived in the upper room.

PASSENHAM is a beautiful and delightful hamlet, close to the Buckinghamshire border and Watling Street and consists of only a few houses, **ST GUTHLAC'S CHURCH,** together with a tithe barn and manor house. Although there was probably a church here around AD921, St Guthlac's was built during the thirteenth and fourteenth centuries and even though Sir Robert Banastre rebuilt the chancel in 1626 the church still retains much of its initial character. Box pews are retained in the church and there are some interesting stalls and misericords of about 1628 with carvings including a monster, lion and unicorn. Look for the unique set of wall paintings in the chancel, recently uncovered and restored, they are part of Banastre's chancel development and are of the evangelists and apostles.

DEANSHANGER has grown out of the parish of Passenham and is now a village in its own right. When part of Passenham the parish church was in that village but in 1853 a church was built in Deanshanger as a chapel of ease. Now dedicated to the **HOLY TRINITY** the church is very simple with a nave and bellcote (no tower), a north aisle and chancel.

The church of the **HOLY TRINITY** is not in the village known today as **CHARWELTON** but several fields away along a gated road where the original village was, and known as Church Charwelton. Alongside the church sitting majestically in the fields is the Manor Farm house and mounds, possibly where the old village was, and to the north west of the church.

The church tower is of the Decorated period and the church has been restored over the years especially the chancel during 1901-04. Look for the two storey porch, one possibility we are told is that the small room above the porch was used by visiting clergy for rest and sleep! On entering the church note the difference in the north and south aisle arcades. The south side has low narrow arches with plain bases and capitals whilst on the north aisle the pillars are slender, the arches higher and there are no capitals. The

richly decorated font is of the fourteenth century, the pulpit is Jacobean and the beautiful brass candelabra are Dutch. Look also to see the lovely line of Victorian oil lamps down the aisles. There are some superb brasses and tombs to the Andrewes family who began as merchants during the fifteenth century. An unusual one for the period is the alabaster wall monument to Thomas Andrewes of 1590, left. This is magnificent and shows him in his armour kneeling before an altar on which his helmet and gauntlets are placed and behind him his two wives and their twelve children all in a different pose. Find the other memorials - they tell an interesting family story.

According to the church booklet by Graham White there is a mystery on the outer wall of the south chapel. There is a scratch dial with the date 1171 and apart from the fact that this dial has all of its rays to its right hand side, the greatest question is of its authenticity. Were these "Arabic Numerals" reading 1171 actually carved in that year, when Roman numerals were thought to be the only form of figures used in England ? Or, could this be one of the country's earliest examples of Arabic numerals ? Perhaps this question will never be answered.

So we come along the A361 to **CHIPPING WARDEN** and the church dedicated to **ST PETER AND ST PAUL** and it is mostly from the Decorated period of church architecture. The nave aisle and arcade is clearly much later than the older side aisles but in the chancel are two tall blocked round arches - do they represent Norman arches? The nave has a lofty fifteenth century arcade and clerestory windows with many carved stone heads supporting the roof. In the north aisle there is a fine niche and a squint opening into a chamber which was evidently the chapel of the Saltonstalls, who built the manor house during the sixteenth century and lie buried in a vault. The east window shows the *Adoration of the Wise Men* and there are scenes from the lives of Peter and Paul.

ALL SAINTS, CROUGHTON is a mixture of Norman and Early English architecture but is a must to visit and explore to see the superb medieval art, said to have been painted around 1280-1300. The south wall depicts scenes from the life of the Virgin Mary and the north wall mainly scenes from the Passion of Christ. The south wall paintings are superb, and the *Flight into Egypt* dazzling and beautiful. This painting is one of several depicting the Nativity of Christ. Angels, shepherds, Herod and the Magi are all there. On the north wall, the story of the Holy Week is portrayed. Clearly shown is the Scourging of Jesus, His Journey to Calvary and the final moments on the cross. These paintings were rediscovered in 1921.

All Saints, Croughton was consecrated about 1080 and continued to develop over the next few centuries. By the end of the fourteenth century much of the present church was in existence and the twentieth century has seen a period of discovery and restoration. Look for the thirteenth century font which has marks where there were hinges, long ago the fonts were locked to keep out witches. The altar in the Lady Chapel was found in the village and restored back into its rightful place. Outside look for a scratch dial on the wall.

CATESBY. A village of two parts, Upper and Lower Catesby. Upper Catesby consists of two rows of houses with the road ending in a gate to a field which leads to the old walled churchyard, but no sign of the church or the priory, founded in 1175. The road that sweeps down from Upper Catesby used to boast a magnificent avenue of elms.
ST MARY'S CHURCH IN LOWER CATESBY was built in 1861-62 and in it are the old piscina and sedilia from the priory. The sedilia has beautiful rich canopied arches and the recesses between them have carved figures - worth visiting to see all this. There is also a Jacobean pulpit and lovely canopy. Close to the church is the old entrance to the priory.

The church of **ST PETER AND ST PAUL, CHACOMBE** is tucked up a lane in an idyllic setting beside the village hostelry. The church is mainly of the Decorated period (thirteenth and fourteenth century), although it has been heavily restored over the last two hundred years. The round Norman font has intersecting arches and on a pillar close by is a carving of a head of a priest with a cross - possibly John Fearneall, the fifteenth century prior. There is an interesting brass slab to Michael Fox (1569) on the chancel floor and, who bought the priory four hundred years ago. Emblems on the slab represent the Holy Trinity, the Arms of the City of London and the Arms of the
Merchant Adventurers. It also commemorates his two wives and seven children.
The priory of Augustinian monks founded in the mid-twelfth century is reputed to be the house now known as The Priory and sits at the foot of the hill. In the grounds are part of the old chapel with gravestones used by the monks and old fish ponds.
In 1982 loose stones were removed from a blocked up window to reveal a wall painting of the martyrdom of Saint Peter. This fourteenth century painting has been restored to encompass its original use - a medieval altar.

BRACKLEY is an old market town separated from Buckinghamshire by the River Ouse which flows nearby. The parish church dedicated to **ST PETER** is situated in the old town with its thirteenth century tower and the west side enriched with arcades and corbels. The church dates back to Norman times and the south doorway is of that period with a medieval crypt and a single central pillar. The worn statues over the west door are attributed to that of St Peter and St Hugh and within the church are a variety of memorials and windows for the visitor to admire.

ASTON-LE-WALLS is a small village on the borders Warwickshire and Oxfordshire and takes its name from an entrenchment which ran along from here to Kirtlington in Oxfordshire a distance of 19 miles. There are several earthworks in the district.
The church of **ST LEONARD** dates from early in the thirteenth century and has a Norman south window and arch in the west wall of the tower and also a Norman font. Also look for the mass dial scratched on the south wall which indicates the great age of the church. The church was restored during the late nineteenth

century. The clerestory was added in the fourteenth century, when also the stone priest with his head on a cushion and hands clasped was laid within the canopied recess. There is a brass of 1609 of Alban Butler with his two wives and 14 children. They were an old Northamptonshire family, two of the descendants, one Charles born in 1750 became a barrister and writer, and another Alban, born in 1711 became a priest and was on the battlefield at Fontenoy as well as becoming a great writer. Also look for the marble bust of Elizabeth Orme with her curious inscription.

Interestingly, although a small village, there is also a Roman Catholic church built in 1827 by the Plowden family who owned the Aston-le-Walls estate until 1920.

We love coming to **AYNHO**, a village steeped in history. The home and estates of the Cartwright family who's line tragically terminated in 1954 when Richard Cartwright and his son were killed in a car accident. The estate was left with problems after the accident and Elizabeth Cartwright Hignett sold the estate in 1960, the family having lived there for three hundred years. The estate is now the property of the Country Households Association.

The Cartwrights were staunch Cromwellians and after the Battle of Naseby the Royalist were fleeing back to Oxford, and when they reached Aynho they vented their fury on the family by burning down the manor and the church. So when you look at the church, dedicated to **ST MICHAEL AND ALL ANGELS**, you will see a tower of the thirteenth century, with the main body of the eighteenth century built in the Grecian style of a chapel, to blend in with the house which partly survived the burning in 1645. We have a building of several architectural periods - Jacobean - Carolean - early eighteenth and nineteenth centuries. When you enter the church it reminds you of a Welsh chapel with its box pews. The walls are painted white but in the right hand corner you will find a little side chapel with the tombs of the Cartwright family. Outside the church is the old preaching cross.

CHARLTON is a small village with no church. This is found in the medieval deserted village of **NEWBOTTLE**. **ST JAMES' CHURCH**, dating from the twelfth century, is situated around a very small cluster of cottages and houses together with a large stone dovecote. The church has a Decorated tower and inside we have a Norman font and an Early English piscina. The pulpit dates from 1567 but one monument in brass is to Peter Dormer of 1555, he is there with his two wives kneeling on his left and right and nineteen children. There is a lovely decorated rood screen probably fourteenth century, and in the south aisle a well decorated wall monument to John and Elizabeth Cresswell. Also admire the east window, the glass showing the Crucifixion and in memory of Lady Cartwright who was buried at Aynho in 1892.

Right: Newbottle Church and above: the interior east end.

Daventry & The Heights

The natural extension of the Cotswolds leads into the Northamptonshire Heights with its undulating pasture, attractive villages and unspoilt countryside. The River Avon begins its journey west into the Bristol Channel and the River Welland its journey north-east to the Wash. Spectacular views over the Welland Valley are more than matched from those along the Jurassic Way - the latter once a busy prehistoric routeway. Ancient villages and churches are all waiting there to be explored and enjoyed.

DAVENTRY, a town perhaps known locally for its connections with the Civil War and the Battle of Naseby. Before Naseby the King's army camped on Borough Hill, an Iron Age hill fort close to the town and Charles I slept in the Wheatsheaf Inn before the battle. However, it is to the imposing and relatively modern town church of **THE HOLY CROSS** that we turn our attention. Built between 1752 and 1758 the structure is mainly Grecian with Roman Doric pillars, supporting low circular arches and a covered roof. Inside are painted galleries and pillars, a groined roof and impressive pulpit. Built of ironstone it is interesting to note that Christianity came to Daventry early and that there was probably a wooden Saxon church on the site or nearby, but certainly there was a church here during the Norman Conquest. The current building is the only eighteenth century church in Northamptonshire. Close by at Preston Capes there was a Cluniac Priory, founded in 1090 and then moving to Daventry in 1107-08.

STAVERTON'S church dedicated to **ST MARY** stands at the southern extremity of the village. Entering the church you will not fail to see and admire the lovely stained glass windows facing you. Many well polished brasses adorn the walls and the vast space of the church holds you in awe and wonderment. The church was built mainly during the fourteenth and fifteenth centuries. The north arcade of the nave has six piers on which are carved curious faces and a large head with its tongue sticking out and grinning! In the north chapel is a handsome monument to Thomas Wyler a gentleman of this parish who died in 1580. The brass shows Thomas and his wife kneeling in prayer with their four sons and six daughters crowded behind.

The first recorded vicar of Staverton was Richard de Staverton in 1220 and, although the church as it stands today is generally not so old, there may be traces of contemporary work, for instance the lancet window near the north west corner. From the outside there is evidence of its replacement by an earlier window, which looks as if it might have been a rounded arched one, and thus would come into the Norman period. So like many of our churches, there is often evidence of earlier buildings on the same or nearby site.

BADBY, recorded in Domesday as Badebi, has a church dedicated to **ST MARY** and sits on a knoll in the centre of the village. The church was built in the fourteenth century (medieval), but was rebuilt early in the seventeenth century, when the pinnacled tower was added and then restored late in the nineteenth century. The ten clerestory windows are quite remarkable for their continuous line without a wall in between. The seventeenth century pulpit is very plain. Visit the church in the Spring and then also go to Badby Woods and see the magnificent display of bluebells.

Lying on the edge of the Northamptonshire Uplands and close to the Warwickshire border **NEWNHAM'S** church dates from the twelfth century although little of this now remains. Dedicated to **ST MICHAEL AND ALL ANGELS** the church has an open tower porch and a fourteenth century spire, together with a similar aged chancel.

Interestingly the church retains some of its box pews and there is a memorial to Letitia Catesby.

Thomas Randolph the poet and dramatist and a contemporary of Ben Johnson, was born in this village and was baptized here on the 15 June 1605.

ST MARY'S CHURCH, BARBY, was largely built from sandstone and dates from the thirteenth century with the first known rector appointed in 1230. The square tower, rebuilt in the eighteenth century has a corbel table of grotesque heads and a sundial over the south doorway. Look for the carvings on the fourteenth century capitals in the north arcades, they have shields and grotesque heads, among them are the arms of the Zouch family who were medieval Lords of the Manor for about three hundred years. Various wall paintings were uncovered during the restoration of 1899. These are very faint and one seems to be the head and legs of a bull. There are some lovely stained glass windows to look at, the east window denotes the Crucifixion, the north chancel depicts the Annunciation and the angel with the shepherds, and there is a First World War memorial window. There is perhaps uniquely a modern carved lectern in the shape of a tree stump and supporting a bronze eagle.

Clipping the border of our county we visit **BRAUNSTON**, a busy canal junction where the Grand Union meets the Oxford Canal. It is here that the Grand Union emerges from the long tunnel and where in the early days of the canal the bargees had to leg it through the tunnel. They laid on their backs on a board, placing their feet on the canal wall and walked the boats through.

Away from the canal you find the church dedicated to **ALL SAINTS** and with an imposing crocketed spire, rebuilt in the Decorated style in 1849. The spire can be seen for miles around. The original church is supposed to have been on the same site and stood for over six hundred years. Explore the church and admire the Norman font, the fourteenth century knight's effigy, an old cross-shaft showing the crucifixion and a lectern with carvings of the Evangelists. Also stop to admire the pulpit built of pink Derbyshire marble and alabaster, and the second font built of similar materials, both added to the church during the late nineteenth century alterations.

ASHBY ST LEDGERS, was, for about 250 years, the home of the Catesby family, who became occupants of the manor in about 1375 and it is during this time that two violent periods in English history took place. William Catesby was a favourite of Richard III but after Richard's defeat at Bosworth in 1485 William was executed and then buried in the church, dedicated to **ST LEODEGARIOUS**. His portrait brass lying within the sixteenth century altar rails shows him with his wife, two sons and daughter. Another William Catesby, a knight and one of Henry VI's carvers is also there. The other violent historical period concerns the Gunpowder Plot and it was here in Ashby St Ledgers that Robert Catesby lived and refusing to attend the Protestant services allied himself to the Roman Catholics. Various stories surround the plot - it was here in the half timbered manor gatehouse house that the Gunpowder Plot was hatched and then when Guy Fawkes was arrested, Catesby and his friends fled back to Ashby to hide, but they continued towards Wales and were tracked down at Holbeach in Staffordshire and executed on 8 November 1605. Further memorials, especially to the Catesby's are found around the church.

Interestingly there are only three other churches in England dedicated to St Leodegarious, Hunstan in Sussex, Wyberton in Leicester and Basford in Nottingham. St Ledger was a pugnacious and political Bishop, who lived in Burgundy in the seventh century and he was canonised and declared a Saint in 685. This is a lovely old church with the original pews of the early fourteenth century, note the shelf on the pews thought to hold books but as there were no printed books when the pews were put in it is assumed they are there as arm rests. Also see the box pews used for the servants and farm workers of the estate. The font is Norman and has a medieval wooden cover. Take a close look at the marvellous and rare three tier Jacobean pulpit. Rare, because of its three tiers - the clerk sat in the bottom seat, the vicar would conduct the service from the middle seat and the preacher would use the top seat. A beautiful rood screen across the aisle is a wonderful piece of carving and well worth a close inspection. There are several wall paintings, the most prolific is the painting of the Black Death, they were discovered during repairs in 1927. There is also a painting on the north wall of the Patron Saint of Travel, St Christopher.

KILSBY, situated on Watling Street and at the junction of the M1 and M45 motorways is at the centre of one of the country's busiest routeways. The church dedicated to **ST FAITH** has a fine tower with a low spire and is mainly of the thirteenth and fourteenth centuries but was heavily restored in 1868-9 and again in 1895.

We find a north aisle and chapel, south aisle and porch, nave, and chancel. The interior is paved and pewed, with a gallery erected at the west end in 1816. The north chapel is separated from the aisle by a low arch, and part of the north aisle is retained as a burial place to the Cowley family of the parish. Moss Cowley left about five acres of land in Lilbourne in 1714, which yielded about ten pounds a year to be expended upon bread for the poor, and educating poor children, and the rent of the "poors close" containing about six acres was distributed yearly amongst the poor at Christmas. In the south aisle there is a beautiful window depicting Simeon with the infant Christ in the Temple, Madonna holding doves and her mother wearing a green robe.

ST MARTIN'S CHURCH, WELTON stands on high ground near the centre of the village and offering splendid views over the valley. The church was built mainly during the medieval period between the thirteenth and sixteenth centuries. The pinnacled tower has a frieze of heads and ornaments and which also run along the top wall of the north aisle. The tub-shaped font is reputed to be Saxon and so the story goes was dragged from East Anglia. The pulpit, an inspirational work was carved by five villagers in 1899, together with the curious poor box, having a hand on top appealing for money! Look around at the monuments and you will find some interesting wall tablets to the Clarkes who lived in Welton Place, now sadly demolished.

WHILTON CHURCH is dedicated to **ST ANDREW** and was of Early English origin but hardly any of the old work remains, except part of the nave arcades. The two upper stages of the tower, the aisle and porch were rebuilt in 1769 and then further restoration and building in 1877.

BROCKHALL, one of Northamptonshire's deserted medieval villages, the peace of which is now incessantly shattered by the M1 motorway which goes straight through the park below the Hall. The church dedicated to **ST PETER AND ST PAUL** is twelfth century and entering the church through the fifteenth century porch you come to the Norman doorway, and look up to notice the way the aisle is separated from the nave by two Norman arches alongside an Early English one. The church was largely rebuilt during the nineteenth century but look for a recess in which is the stone to Peter de Thurlston, a thirteenth century rector. Looking around you will find a variety of wall monuments to the Thorntons. One of the Thorntons was the local squire and rector for 63 years, and there is a window in his memory. Finally, as you leave look for the scratch dial on the south-east corner wall.

NORTON village, only one mile from Daventry is very proud of its treasured colourful tomb - Sir Richard Knightley and his second wife Lady Elizabeth Seymour who was daughter of the Duke of Somerset, Lord Protector of England in the reign of Edward II. Sir Richard would use Norton Hall when he wanted a change from Fawsley! He was knighted at Fotheringhay and present at the execution of Mary Queen of Scots in 1587. The church dedicated to **ALL SAINTS** is thirteenth century with a battlemented tower and medieval arcades of six arches on each side of the nave. There is a large round thirteenth century font with four heads projecting out and several monuments to the Bretons and Botfields whose families both lived in the hall. The Breton's succeeded the Knightley's in 1615 and lived there for two hundred years before the Botfield's came.

DODFORD parish, adjacent to a tributary of the river Nene gets its name from a ford over the river and in May 1664 the water rose eight feet in a short space of time causing floods throughout the village.

The church dedicated to **ST MARY** stands on a gentle hill between the village and the A5 Watling Street. The north aisle is Early English, the body about a century later and the chancel was rebuilt in the reign of George III. The ornate font is reputed to be Norman, as is the south wall and windows. One of the earliest monuments is that of a member of the De Keynes family, a knight in banded mail dressed as he might have appeared in battle during the thirteenth century. You will see that he has his legs crossed, denoting that he has been to the crusades. Now look to the north wall and see the ornate pointed arch with bold deep mouldings. Here are two effigies,

one of wood, believed to be Wentiliana the grandaughter and Elisabeth the daughter of Sir William de Keynes who died in 1375 and 1376 respectively. The gentleman on the stone plinth at the end is Sir John Cressy who died in 1443 note his legs are not crossed, he rests his head on the head-dress of his armour. Explore the monuments and see the story of the de Keynes family unfold - its fascinating.

The old church of **BOUGHTON** dedicated to **ST JOHN THE BAPTIST** stands on a green about half a mile from the village, but all that remains is a supported arch and some stones. This was the site of the first village and the site of Boughton Green Fair, first established in 1351. The current church dedicated to the same saint lies in the centre of the new village surrounded by a variety of residential property and began life as a chantry chapel, probably during the sixteenth century. The tower is late Perpendicular with repairs and additions around 1600-1700. The body of the church being restored around the beginning of the nineteenth century and consecrated by the Bishop of Peterborough on the 6th March 1808.

Turning off the A508 north of Brixworth we find the village of **SCALDWELL**. The church dedicated to **ST PETER AND ST PAUL** stands on a hillside almost in the centre of the village and consists of a chancel with a north aisle and chapel, nave, south aisle with a vestry, and south porch and west tower. The church was extensively restored in 1863, but there is still evidence of good Norman work in the tower. Four pinnacles were later added to the tower and a lovely sanctus bell-cote survives. The font is thirteenth century and in the churchyard are the remains of an old preaching cross.

ST ANDREW'S CHURCH, OLD close to Brixworth and Pitsford Reservoir dates from the end of the thirteenth century and has a Perpendicular tower. Entering the church you cannot help but sense and see the vastness of the building. Look up to see the nave roof with beautiful stone carved angels representing the twelve apostles. In the north porch note the two very old windows, much older than the porch and is thought to have come from another part of the church. There are some unusual carvings around the north door and the door itself is very old. In the south aisle window we find medieval glass. There is a man with the devil on his back, or so it should be. It is possible that Cromwell's men smashed the glass and it has been difficult to piece together, having found the glass in 1874 wrapped in a piece of cloth and under the floor boards. There are lovely carved bench ends in the choir stalls. While you walk around the church have a look at the south wall, does it lean back ? The people of the village are making wonderful kneelers all containing their own stories. One of the kneelers will measure seventeen and a half feet across the altar rails

Medieval tombstone, Old.

and will depict Noah and the Ark, with the animals making their way to the Ark and also Noah's three sons and their wives. It is expected that over 5,000 hours work will go into the project and it is hoped to be completed in time for the Millennium. Look around the kneelers to find a twentieth century illustration of an old Rover car. There is the old chest down at the west end where they stored the village records. There are no pews in the church they have been replaced by chairs.

ST PETER'S, WALGRAVE, left, stands on elevated ground in the centre of the village and was mainly built during the fourteenth century. The square tower gives way to a beautiful lofty broach spire. In

1867-8 the spire was partly rebuilt and the church restored, also adding the clerestory windows. In the chancel there are mural tablets to Mountague Lane and Samuel Harris. The font is old and consists of a circular bowl with a moulded top on a pillared stem. In a glass case there is a chained bible of 1611 and a "Book of Homilies" of 1676 the case is made up of old pew ends. The chancel screen has gone from the chancel arch and part of it is now in the tower arch. Look for the the vine carvings on the screen which dates from the fifteenth century. The timbered roof has disappeared but you can see where it used to be, for up on the chancel wall are the old bosses elegantly carved by fourteenth century craftsmen. John Williams who was rector at St Peters later became Archbishop of York during Charles I's reign.

HANNINGTON village, about mid-way between Northampton and Kettering has a unique church, with two naves. The church of **ST PETER AND ST PAUL** was built in the thirteenth century and there are two pillars down the centre of the aisle supporting an arcade of three arches which support the roof, thus creating a bisected nave. One of only three other similar

designs in England, according to *'The Buildings of England, Northamptonshire' by Nikolaus Pevsner*. The round headed south doorway is possibly late Norman design and from an earlier church, whilst the chancel roof is covered in hand made tiles. Across the chancel arch there used to be a fourteenth century screen of oak with doors and panels but this has now been moved to the tower arch forming the belfry. The octagonal oak pulpit is a similar carving and age, the top being cut from the trunk of a huge oak tree. The north porch has an interesting notice reminding readers that during medieval times the church porch was the place where much of the civil business was undertaken. Here the coroner would sit, executors make public payments, marriage banns were published and marriage vows made. Here also the baptismal service commenced and entered the church to the font, the door was sometimes called the Christening door.

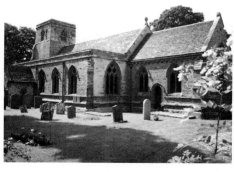

PITSFORD, adjacent to the reservoir has a beautiful church dating back to the Normans. **ALL SAINTS**, in an old part of the village, but with limited modern development around, has a superb Norman doorway - quite remarkable for its tympanum showing a weird animal struggling with an armed man with animals around. Does the carving represent St George and the Dragon, or St Michael the Archangel in combat

with the devil?! The doorway is worth further exploration to see the inner zig-zag frame with grotesque faces and heads all around. The fourteenth century carved font and thirteenth century tower remain but the church over the years has been restored and refurbished. A modern development are the carvings of the 1930's on the pillars of the nave. These show the twelve Apostles. Interestingly the old village situated north of the church was completely destroyed by fire in 1619.

ST MARY AND ALL SAINTS, HOLCOT is situated in the middle of the village which is fairly close to Pitsford Reservoir. The medieval church has a fourteenth century battlemented tower with four huge gargoyles. The church is probably well known in the area for its abundance of medieval paintings, which depict scenes from the New Testament including the Ascension, Pentecost and the Passion. Over the years the parishioners have held numerous fund raising events to enable continued restoration of these paintings. Although faded the painting in the north aisle shows the Martydom of Thomas Becket. In the south side of the churchyard there is a fifteenth century limestone cross and it is likely that the cross originally stood at the junction of the Brixworth - Moulton crossroads.

MOULTON, on the A43 to Kettering and although a suburb of Northampton and four miles from the town centre, has fought over the years to keep its own identity. The church of **ST PETER AND ST PAUL** was built out of Northamptonshire ironstone during the Norman and medieval periods of architecture. A small wooden church probably existed in Moulton towards the end of the seventh century and was burnt down by the Danish invaders. The church was laid to ruin in 1265 during the Baron's War and in 1298 rebuilding began. The three main doorways are all fourteenth century and the nave has four round Norman arches and a fragment of a Norman window above them. Moulton like many villages and churches often has evidence of an earlier settlement or church. Moulton church has the fragments of a Saxon cross shaft indicating that the site was used, as mentioned, for worship earlier than the present church. Also look for the thirteenth century broken coffin lid with a cross decoration. The church continued

with restoration especially during the nineteenth century.

Moulton is also perhaps more widely known for its associations with William Carey who formed the Baptist Missionary Society in 1792. Carey was a missionary in India from 1793 until his death in 1834 and became Baptist Pastor in Moulton in 1786 having first moved to the village a year earlier.

After St Martins at Canterbury **ALL SAINTS AT BRIXWORTH**, together with a handful of others, is probably one of the oldest churches in England and certainly the most outstanding Saxon church in England. There is speculation as to when the original church was built. One theory is that the monks of Medeshamstede, later known as Peterborough, built the church in AD680. The other theory was that the church was built about AD750 by King Ethelbald of Mercia in honour of his friend Boniface. The latest theory would fit in well with the 'relic', thought to be the larynx bone of St. Boniface, which used to be found in an iron cage by the pulpit.

Situated on a hill, Brixworth church dominates the surrounding countryside. Brixworth was probably an important place in Roman times and certainly a substantial amount of Roman material has been used in building the church. The church is situated close to the site of a Roman villa.

Entering the church the visitor will be impressed by the quiet spacious solemnity with eyes being drawn to look through the nave and to the altar in the apse. The magnificent great arch separating the nave from the choir was put there in about 1400. Perhaps the easiest eye-catching characteristics are the Roman tiles which helped shape many of the north and south Saxon arches inside the church and also above the Norman south door. This entrance also has examples of Norman pillars and just inside the front door is a wonderful example of a Saxon eagle's head. The stair-turret, probably added to the tower during the ninth and tenth centuries, is one of only a few left in the country, and completely blocked the west door. Look at the tower and notice how the stair-turret rises above the line of the old Saxon tower. The additional tower of red bricks and spire was probably added about 1350 and clearly shows the change in window style from the round Norman arch to the Early English and decorated style. This contrasting style is also shown in the Lady Chapel on the south side. The circular apse at the east end of the church is famous for its sunken passage running around the outside and called the ambulatory. Originally it had a vaulted roof, with access from inside the church, and led to the crypt chapel underneath the apse. The treasures and the relic would have been kept in this chapel.

Return to the road through the churchyard and look back on this magnificent building - a unique example of Anglo-Saxon architecture. Close to the road are the old village stocks and part of the fourteenth century market cross.

SPRATTON village on the main Northampton to Market Harborough road has an old church, dedicated to **ST ANDREW**, probably dating back to the Saxon period. The tower is late Norman as is the doorway with zig-zag carvings and grotesque heads. The nave has four Norman north arches with rich carvings on their capitals and the south arcades are Early English. The spire rising from the battlements of the Norman tower is fourteenth century and a screen added the following century separates the north aisle from the chapel. There are two arches in the chancel also from this period. Under one of these lies the tomb of Sir John Swinford, 1371. Sir John lies in his chain mail, plate armour, with his feet on an animal and his head on his helmet. His hands are together in prayer. The font is Norman and there are some lovely carvings on the ends of the choir stalls - look for a choirboy, a man playing a pipe, an angel and a bishop.

There is an old preaching cross in the churchyard, but it is thought that this is not in its original position. Also in the churchyard as you enter on the right are two table top tombs dated 1500. So valuable are these that they are now under a preservation order.

ST MICHAEL'S CHURCH CREATON, situated in the village a few yards off the Leicester road out of Northampton, dates back to the thirteenth century. The small tower is original and there is a late twelfth century doorway still retaining its leaf carvings.

ST HELEN'S, THORNBY, originally built during the thirteenth to fifthteenth centuries still retains its tower and battlements from that era, together with its early piscina and carved Norman font. It has, however, over the years been heavily restored losing many of its other artefacts.

A very rural village tucked away about ten miles from Northampton and close to Creaton, **COTTESBROOKE** retains that 'old world charm'. Cottesbrooke Hall keeps much of its manorial charm and is open to the public on certain days in the years. The church of **ALL SAINTS** dates from around 1220 but like all churches has developed over the years and interestingly has a carefully restored three-tier pulpit, fifteenth century roof timbers revealed during restoration and box pews. Explore the church memorials, some destruction of these occurred when Cromwell's army was in the area (Naseby is nearby), but there is a table tomb of black and white marble on which lie Sir John Langham and his wife. Sir John is wearing his alderman's robes and he was made a baronet by Charles II. Also close by is the memorial to John Rede who bought the manor from Sir John. Both these memorials are seventeenth century. An interesting story associated with Cottesbrooke concerns Parson Legard who was a keen horseman and would ride with the local hunt, and during a funeral, having tied his horse to the gate and seeing the hunt ride past, left the corpse at the graveside and joined them!!

Northamptonshire has many unusual churches, normally found in the centre of the village or on a hill, but occasionally one is found along a track and in a field. **ALL SAINTS AT HOLDENBY** is approached through the gardens of Holdenby House, more famous for holding Charles I prisoner there in 1647, or down a trackway from the village. Although there are occasional services in the church, it belongs to the 'Redundant Churches' and is looked after by the English Heritage. The tranquillity and calm within the church, which is built of local sandstone, is in stark contrast to the history that the crumbling walls would tell. The church is not a ruin, but loose mortar, dust and cracks tell their own story. It is a fascinating church with the local wildlife having taken over, and the only regular prayers perhaps coming from the hungry sparrows as they hunt for food around the memorials. There are many of these around the church, perhaps the most impressive one being the chancel arch upon which stands the cross flanked by two Roman soldiers. Naturally, within the church, there are memorials to the Holdenby family. On the floor of the east end of the south aisle there is an alabaster slab dedicated to William Holdenby, who died in 1490, and also to his wife Margaret. Next to this is also a late thirteenth century coffin lid and two marble memorial slabs with brass inscriptions. One of these is said to have been used as a memorial to Elizabeth Hatton, heiress of the Holdenbys. Further memorials and brasses are found in many parts of the church.

Adorning the nave and aisle walls are seven painted texts, each one with a strapwork surround. The texts are probably Elizabethan as they are taken from a 'Bishop's Bible' of 1568. They were discovered and repainted in 1862. Three were added later, *the Lord's Prayer, the Creed and the Ten Commandments.*

The church dates back to the first half of the fourteenth century although additions have been made throughout the centuries. There's a link with Canons Ashby as Dryden designed the rebuilding of the chancel in 1843-45. It contains a fine set of stalls with simple miserichords which, although restored, were originally fifteenth century. The chancel walls were painted in 1868 and include angels flanking the upper east window.

CHURCH BRAMPTON is one of two villages, the other one is Chapel Brampton which sits on the A50 road just up the hill from Church Brampton. The church, built predominately during the Decorated period, is dedicated to **ST BOTOLPH'S** and consists of an embattled tower, and a chancel, rebuilt in 1860. Look for the corbel table of tiny heads around the tower and monster gargoyles looking out from the aisles. The church still retains many arches and a north and south doorway built during the thirteenth century and over the south doorway are the carved Royal Arms of Edward III. Finally look for the strange brass, a memorial to Jone Furnace showing her in a shroud engraved with the outline of a skeleton. There is a wonderful old and ancient parish chest, probably dating from the late thirteenth century and which is bound on the lid, front, and sides with iron work. Immediately outside the church is the shaft of a medieval preaching cross.

LOWER HARLESTONE just outside Northampton is bisected by the A428 leading through to Crick and the M1. **UPPER HARLESTONE,** also a small village stretches out about a mile off the main road. Both villages are on the estate owned by the Spencers of Althorp House, the early home of the late Diana Princess of Wales.

The church of **ST ANDREW** lies between the two villages and was mainly built during the Decorated (1280-1350) period of architecture. There is a late Norman font with

carved heads and also look for the carved heads in the sanctuary. Also look at the beautiful black oak carved pulpit, right, to find saints, the Ascension, Christ, the sun and moon. As you stand in the main aisle and look towards the altar, you will notice where the old roof used to be, also by turning round you can see the old late seventeenth century musicians gallery at the rear of the church. The lych gate was a gift from the Duchess of Grafton, given to the church in 1903 commemorating Queen Victoria's Diamond Jubilee.

The church of **ST MARY THE VIRGIN, GREAT BRINGTON** has become a very popular tourist attraction since the death of Diana, Princess of Wales and it is necessary to co-ordinate your visit on the days set aside for this. Information is available from the Tourist Information Centre in Northampton. However a visit to the church is essential to see and admire the wealth and pageantry of the Spencer Chapel. The church at Great Brington is used by the Spencer Estate and over the years money has been provided for repairs, improvements and developments. Although a church was recorded in Brington in the Domesday Book, the existing one was built around 1200 and added to in subsequent years. The initial building comprised the tower, north and south aisles, nave and chancel. During the fourteenth century the south

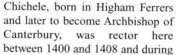

aisle was rebuilt and then during the following century alterations and additions in the Perpendicular style were inserted. In 1508 Sir John Spencer purchased Althorp and by 1514 had added the Spencer Chapel in the north. The chapel contains a series of monuments to the family. There are five full-length effigies recumbent on canopied altar tombs and three of these divide the chapel from the chancel. These richly, colourful, ostentatious tombs offer splendour, unparalleled anywhere else in the county. Henry Chichele, born in Higham Ferrers and later to become Archbishop of Canterbury, was rector here between 1400 and 1408 and during

his ministry the first in a series of five bench ends were carved. There are many bench end carvings found in the church, and these continued through to the last in the series in 1903. An interesting local tradition declares that Charles I made his communion in St Mary's during his imprisonment at Holdenby House in 1647. Look also in the church for the tombs of the Washington brothers - Robert and Laurence. They are the sons of Lawrence Washington who built Sulgrave Manor. Richard and Laurence came to live in the Bringtons around 1600. Robert, buried in the nave has two brasses on his tombstone, whilst Laurence is in the north aisle, but you need to remove a wooden cover to see this.

The ancient church of **ST MARY'S, EAST HADDON** stands near the centre of the village and was remodelled during the fourteenth century, having originally been a Norman building. The top of the tower was added in 1673. The chancel arch rests on Norman pillars

and the lovely Norman font is sculptured with a man holding two serpents - possibly symbolic of baptismal victory over sin.

GUILSBOROUGH, just off the Leicester road and about ten miles from Northampton is a fairly large village with a church dedicated to **ST ETHELREDA**. Both the tower and spire date from the thirteenth and fourteenth centuries and are the only sections of the exterior fabric of the church remaining from the early periods. Although beautifully fitted the church has been extensively restored inside. There are many Burne-Jones memorials in memory of Countess Spencer, wife of the fourth earl who died in Guilsborough Hall in 1877. The church is worth exploring to see the corbels on the nave arches, the Last Supper scene across the front of the altar. The poet Wordsworth is said to have stayed at the vicarage when visiting his friend Sikes.

ST DENY'S CHURCH, RAVENSTHORPE dates back to the thirteenth century, with the west tower and arcades still remaining from that period, despite rebuilding and restoration during the nineteenth century. Underneath the communion table there used to be a large chest, covered in thin plates of metal crossing each other at right angles, and in this was found a breast plate and gauntlets which hang in the vestry. These may have come from the Battle of Naseby. There is a piscina in the south aisle; a narrow arched entrance for the rood loft still remains at the south east end of the nave; and the entrance to the chancel from the nave is through an ancient and beautifully carved wooden screen. Some of the original seats still remain, with their square carved ends. The Jacobean pulpit is dated St George's Day April the 23rd 1619. Look closely at the round font which is reputed to be Norman and see if you can see the carving of a head and hind quarters of a horse.

NASEBY, better known for the decisive battle fought during the Civil War in 1645, and for the two monuments and museum recognising this, has, as you would expect, memories and artefacts associated with the battle. Inside the church of **ALL SAINTS** is 'Cromwell's Table' reputed to have been in the local pub (now Shuckborough House), and used on the eve of the battle by the Royalists. Another story suggests that Cromwell dined at the table after the battle. The ten foot long table is found in the north aisle and which ever story is true, the table could certainly tell a tale or two. Another legend is that Cromwell stabled his horses in the church on the eve of the battle. The church was possibly in existence in Saxon times as there is supposed to be a Saxon stone carved with a cross set in the tower inside the church and in the room at the foot of the tower there is also a lid of a Saxon coffin found in the churchyard. There is also evidence of a Norman building with a circular font from this period. The main church fabric was built between 1200 and 1550. Look for the gargoyles around the tower and find amongst others, eagles.

SIBBERTOFT, straddling Naseby and the battlefield would have many a tale to tell about the Civil War and King Charles who raised his standard at Moot Hill, to the east of the village. The church dedicated to **ST HELEN** records its first rector in 1220 and although the church was built between the thirteenth and sixteenth centuries it may go back further. Extensive restoration in 1862-63 has left little evidence of previous years. The old rood-loft stairway, now used to give access to the pulpit, and a brass to Anthony Atkins, who died on the 20 September 1564, with inscriptions in Latin and English are both worth seeing.

Originally **HOLLOWELL** was a hamlet in the Guilsborough parish but in 1840 Kempthorne built the church of **ST JAMES** in the Lancet style with a small bell-cote and a high pitched roof. The interior is very neat and open with carved seats. Hollowell sits on the side of the hill overlooking Hollowell Reservoir and just off the Northampton to Leicester road.

LONG BUCKBY, larger than most villages is unique, in that passing through the parish is the A5 Watling Street, the M1 motorway, The Grand Union Canal and the main line railway - almost all forms of transport.

The church of St Lawrence is built of Northamptonshire ironstone. The tower was built during the Early English period with the remainder of the church being of the Decorated period. During the nineteenth century the church was restored and in 1849 the church had five bells, the tenor being inscribed, '*If at my sound you don't prepare, You're not inclined to come to prayer'*. Look around the church for memorials and gargoyles and in particular for the memorial to Eliza Gardner who died instantly when drunks knocked on the door of her house, giving her a fright that was fatal.

ST PETER AND ST PAUL, WATFORD was mainly built during the Early English and Decorated periods of architecture, with the tower being added the following century. The south porch is rather interesting as the moulding is from the Decorated style and yet there is dog tooth ornamentation. Look inside for the three sedilia and stand and admire the high arches and the large west window. There are several monuments to the Clark family who were the owners of the manor, Watford Court. Sir Robert Clarke who died in 1649 had a very simple tablet and to the left of him a further George Clarke who died in 1689.

WEST HADDON church is dedicated to **ALL SAINTS** and consists of a nave and side aisles, chancel and south porch. It has an embattled tower which once had a spire, and having fallen into decay was taken down in 1648. The porch through which we enter the church is 300 years old and the door, complete with studs and ironwork twice its age, having been there since the fourteenth century. Inside the doorway is the magnificent square Norman font carved out of one solid piece of stone depicting scenes from the life of Christ. These wonderful scenes, possibly unique, represent the Nativity, the Baptism of Christ, Entry into Jerusalem on Psalm Sunday and Christ in Glory between the Eagle of St John and the Angel of St Matthew. The east window depicts a glowing scene of Gethsemane, showing three disciples sleeping, Judas with his money and Our Lord and the Archangel Gabriel. It is worth visiting the church to see the window and font but there is also evidence of the medieval church with piscinas, arcades, clerestory windows and the south wall.

WINWICK village lies tucked away between West Haddon and Yelvertoft. The church dedicated to **ST MICHAEL** is one of the county's cruciform churches and it consists of a nave, chancel, transepts, porch and the embattled tower which is Early Perpendicular and possibly the best part of the building. The chancel and transepts are also Early English and the nave and porch are in the Decorated style. Look around to find the gargoyles staring at you from the tower. Inside there used to be an old barrel organ which is currently undergoing repair and is then to be presented to the Northampton museum.

ALL SAINTS, YELVERTOFT is perhaps best know for its three aisles, the extra one being in the south and for its wonderful tomb of John Dycson who was rector of the parish between 1439 and 1445 His monument occupies nearly the whole north side of the chancel. Within the canopied recess lies the priest on a low tomb-chest and two angels at his pillow. Look for the sedilia. It is said that Cromwell's army sharpened their swords on the worn pillars of the sedilia.

CRICK, close to Junction 18 on the M1, has a beautiful church dedicated **ST MARGARET OF ANTIOCH** and is built of yellow sandstone, although the tower is made from red Warwickshire stone. The church dates from the thirteenth century and at one time seems to have been ornamented throughout with rich painted glass, and the walls decorated with fresco paintings; some remains of the latter were discovered during the repairs in the early 1800's. The sedilia and piscina are of a very rich design, and evidently of the original fabric. The Norman font has the bowl resting on three monsters and the priest's door has the possible Norman curved arch with carved tympanum, (see Pitsford). Look around both inside and outside the church to find beautiful carvings, look especially for a winged horse and a green man, (a head with branches and leaves coming out of his mouth). The Norman font rests on three kneeling figures and look for the portrait of Archbishop Laud by Van Dyke. The Archbishop who was martyred in 1644 was rector of the parish from 1642-44.

LILBOURNE, situated in beautiful Avon countryside lies just off the A5 Watling Street and close to the Warwickshire border. There was a lot of Roman activity in this area and the church of **ALL SAINTS** is close to two motte and bailey castle sites, the mounds of which are still there. The church dates from the thirteenth and fourteenth centuries, although recently two old Saxon doorways have been discovered. The rood steps remain in the south aisle and there is a sanctus bellcote over the nave gable, the bell is still preserved in the church. Look around for some lovely carved heads; the font is modern by church dates but there are also remnants of the old Norman font.
Look around the outside of the walls and find different 'rubble type' stone used to build the church. This supports the theory that the church was possibly built with stone from the castle which stood across the road.

STANFORD ON AVON. We were astounded on our first visit to the village - the beauty, peace and quietness together with the thatched cottages built of Northamptonshire ironstone and an 'old worldleness' was like turning the clock back fifty years. We did not know such places still existed! As you would guess in such a small village the church of **ST NICHOLAS** is redundant and is maintained by the 'British Heritage'. It has over the last few years

been magnificently restored to its ancient beauty, saving the fantastic monuments to the Cave and Bray families. Sir Roger Cave built nearby Stanford Hall between 1697 and 1700 and there are many superb memorials to the family for you to explore and see. All interesting, but also the one to Edward Verney, right, who died in 1896 has a Zulu shield, showing that he fought in South Africa during the Zulu War. The Verneys have also lived at the hall.

Lady Braye, 1862.

The church was mainly built between 1300 and 1350 and, as already said, recently restored. There are no pews and with its slender piers it takes on the look of a miniature cathedral and the clerestory windows make it very light and airy. It has a wonderful wooden roof with tie beams. The font carved with simple patterns is from the fourteenth century. The stained glass windows are magnificent dating from the early fourteenth century through to the sixteenth century, and again is worth visiting to see these. Look towards the west end and see the magnificent organ standing on pillars. It is said that it came from Whitehall

Palace. When Oliver Cromwell did not like it at the Palace he had it removed, eventually making its way to Stanford.

The small village of **COLD ASHBY** lies just off the main Northampton to Leicester road and a few miles south of the border. Arriving at the church of **ST DENIS** you cannot fail to be impressed by the magnificent Victorian stone lych gate, dated 1883. The church was mainly built during the Early English (1200-1300) period, although there is possibly Saxon carved stonework in the doorway of the vestry, and there is a Norman north doorway. St Denis also has one of the oldest bells in the country, inscribed with the date 1317 and a Latin prayer to the Madonna. The huge font is medieval and very beautiful. Look at the interesting and delightful stained glass windows depicting possible scenes from the church.

ARTHINGWORTH village close to the A508 and just south of Market Harborough has a late Norman church, although it has had a great deal of restoration over the years - mainly during the nineteenth century. The south arcade of **ST ANDREW'S** has one original circular pier with scalloped capital but the second pier seems to be nineteenth century and there also appears to be the large remains of the thirteenth century south chapel. There is a good marble monument to a Mrs Jekyll who died in 1775 and within the monument there is an angel with a quill.

HARRINGTON village situated seven miles west of Kettering has wonderful views across the countryside and valley, with the thirteenth century church of **ST PETER AND ST PAUL** outside the village on the Thorpe Underwood road. The church was remodelled in the nineteenth century and the tower added at the end of the south transept in 1809. The church has a beautifully carved medieval screen and the chancel tiles are the original ones. Harrington is the proud owner of a seventeenth century vamping horn, one of only two in the county and only six or eight in the country (number depends on which book you read)! Braybrooke has the other in the county and they were used like a megaphone for summoning people to church or to help the choir. It is thought that many of the victims of the Battle of Naseby were buried in the churchyard.

ST CATHERINE'S CHURCH, DRAUGHTON is situated in a small village just off the main road and about midway along the Northampton to Market Harborough A508. The church has a flat twelfth century tower with a small rounded arch west window. The simply built church, still retaining much of the early architecture, had the chancel added in 1885. The font dated around 1800 has a carved serpent winding its way up the stem with an apple in its jaw - rather a strange symbol. Is this symbolic of the devil and Eve tempted by the apple in the Garden of Eden and Baptism being the act of washing away these sins at the start of a new life?

Close to the Leicestershire border **ST JOHN THE BAPTIST, EAST FARNDON** was built during the Decorated and Perpendicular periods of architecture and retains much of the original fabric even though it has been restored over time. One of the windows represents Faith, Hope and Charity and is a memorial to a rector of the parish.
There is also an unusual brass to the Rector Daniel Halford with his portrait, an hourglass, a skull and a laurel wreath.

BRAYBROOKE CHURCH dedicated to **ALL SAINTS** was mainly built during the Early English and early Decorated period (thirteenth and fourteenth centuries), and contains many artefacts worth exploring. The square font is Norman with a cross and figure holding two fishes carved into the stone. There are traces of wall paintings in the south aisle including possibly a priest. Look closely to find the

main treasure which is undoubtedly the well preserved oak figure of Sir Thomas de Latymer, who lived in the castle and who went crusading from here during the fourteenth century. The carving comes from a single piece of wood.

Close by in a recess in the wall is the huge carving of a head of a man. The Griffins who followed the Latymers at the castle have a strange Elizabethan monument, the artist having introduced griffins crawling all over it! The Perpendicular screen is also carved with animals and birds and although damage was obviously a work of art. Also found in the church is a vamping horn, one of only two found in Northamptonshire, now in the local museum. Made of brass and like a megaphone, it is five foot long with a diameter of 25 inches at the larger end and it might have been used to summon parishioners to church as they could often be heard for up to a mile away, but it is more probable that it served to accompany the choir or singers.

The church of **ST HELEN** sits proudly on the hill, just outside the village of **GREAT OXENDON** and looks into Leicestershire. It is thought that the original church was probably situated in the old village. After the Black Death struck in the original village the settlement was moved. The church font is Norman and there is thirteenth and four-

teenth century arcading and a restored chancel arch. Over the years St Helen's has been restored and in 1968 during the Harvest Service the vicar preached from under an umbrella, as the church roof had collapsed. This resulted in the church being closed until 1976 when, after great efforts by the parishioners it was again repaired and reopened.

The Rev John Morton, author of the, "Natural History of Northamptonshire" was instituted rector in 1706, published his work in 1712 and was buried here in 1737.

MARSTON TRUSSELL, situated close to Market Harborough and just inside the county the village is named after the Lords of the Manor, the Trussells, who were lords here soon after the Norman Conquest. The church dedicated to **ST NICHOLAS** seems to have been built during the 1300-1500 period, has a Perpendicular tower with windows, arcades and doorways built during the late thirteenth and fourteenth centuries. The north porch is built of solid timbers and inside we find a chest carved from one trunk of oak around the time of the Magna Carta. Look for the memorial tomb of Mark Brewster. He left money for

the poor of the village and forty pounds for a new bell. He was a Freeman of the Ironmongers Company and is reputed to have made his fortune as a pirate in Russia. He came to England to retire but the Tsar's men found him and returned him to Russia for trial, where he was found guilty and executed in Moscow in 1612.

A sad story emerging from the Battle of Naseby tells of a group of Cavaliers who were escaping from the battle. When they were caught hiding in the churchyard they were slain by Cromwell's men and buried in the churchyard.

Above: Crest on south wall and below: The south porch

The church of **ST MICHAEL, HASELBECH** dates back from the thirteenth century and although the west tower is probably of a later date the west windows of the aisles are probably original ones, whilst others have been remodelled. Although the church has been restored many of the old arcades have been retained and the eastern parts seem to be nineteenth century. The church has three screens; a fine metal screen at the chancel steps, a lovely oak carved screen at the west end and a further iron screen is part of a wall memorial. The pulpit is Jacobean. there is a coffin bier and stocks at the west end of the church and two beautiful two seated sedilia close to the altar.

In the south aisle there is a wall monument to Charles Bowyer Ismay, a game hunter. Look around the north side of the churchyard for his tomb and to see a frieze of animals.

ALL SAINTS, CLIPSTON was probably built originally during the Norman period, although little evidence of this remains. There are two Norman doorways, one through which church is entered and the second leading into the south chapel, which is also divided from the chancel by a thirteenth century arch. There is also a Norman font, found in the churchyard. Look for Queen Victoria's head looking down from the west window of the tower. Look further around the church to find monuments to the Buswell family, a family of London merchants. Sir George Buswell founded the hospital for poor people and the school (1673).

A few miles from the Leicester border on the Northampton to Leicester road lies the small village of **KELMARSH**. The church of **ST DENYS** is a short distance from the village out along the Clipston road and appears to have been built during the Perpendicular period. The chancel was restored during the Victorian era, 1874, by

Below: Old tomb, Kelmarsh

Mr and Mrs Naylor who owned Kelmarsh Hall and reputedly brought the colourful marble from Rome, which you can see so vividly today all around the chancel. There are some lovely carved bench ends. Also look up to the hammer beam roof and see the

golden angels. Look for a wall monument in the north chapel to Sir John Hanbury who died in 1639 and to his wife. It is a large standing monument as they kneel in prayer facing one another across a prayer desk.

LAMPORT CHURCH OF ALL HALLOWS was built during the twelfth and thirteenth centuries, and largely reconstructed in the seventeenth and eighteenth centuries. All Hallows contains the Isham family chapel built in 1672. The Isham family having lived in Isham Hall from 1560. It is also interesting to find in the churchyard the tomb of Sir Gyles Isham, the twelfth and last Baronet. He died in 1976 and you will find his tomb in the east, by the path leading to the eighteenth century rectory.

The church is dominated by its bulky squat west tower, the base of which was originally built during the late Norman period and then added to during the thirteenth century, although there may have been a Saxon church earlier. The church has been restored over the years but you can find Norman work in the west window in the tower and there is a Norman doorway beneath. The arcades and clerestory windows are fourteenth century. There is a lovely fifteenth century cross which is reputed to have belonged to the chaplain to Mary Tudor. He died in 1546 and it eventually came into the Isham collection. The cross has the Lord, Madonna and St John in wonderful enamelling all laid on bronze and approximately two feet long, but owing to its value and treasure it is kept in safe keeping.

MAIDWELL village, just north of Brixworth on the Market Harborough road once had two churches - St Mary and St Peter, the latter having disappeared around 1540 and being situated close to the residential housing of St Peter's Close.

ST MARY'S CHURCH was originally built during the Norman period and there is a plain Norman arch in the south doorway and the tower has some Norman work inside, although todays structure is mainly thirteenth century with the upper stage dated 1706. Brought from the old church is a magnificent monument, a beautifully painted tomb of Baron Gorges, Lord Dundalk and to his wife Catherine. She lies in an unusual position on a higher level than the Lord and lying in an elaborate recess. In the chancel are two battered figures of men in armour, one of which is supposed to have been Sir John Seaton who died in Jerusalem in 1396 and whose remains are interned here.

Rockingham Castle Corby & Kettering

After rising on the Northamptonshire Heights the River Welland flows north into a broad valley, acting as the county border along much of the north and west. Rockingham Forest majestically overlooks the valley together with many of the villages and it is the forest which takes its name from the royal Castle. Most of the forest has been felled, and today is a patchwork of farms and small villages with only Corby and Kettering as the main towns.

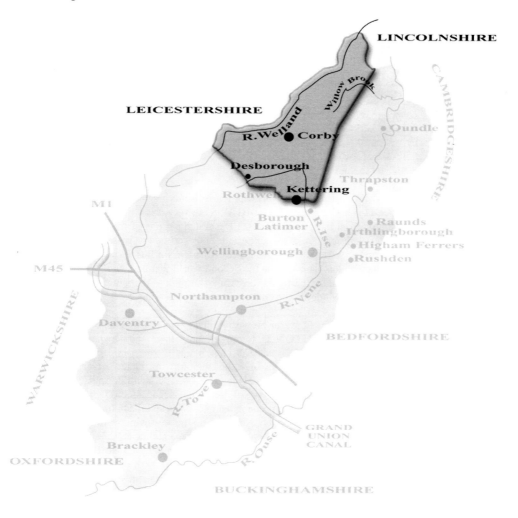

ST LEONARD'S, THORPE MALSOR, built of Northamptonshire ironstone during the late thirteenth and early fourteenth centuries was restored in 1877. The church retains much of its old style, a carved font, the west tower and several windows are all from the initial building. Look for the angels holding up the roof, a carved pelican bench-end and what is possibly a priest's room over the porch. Also find the memorials to the Maunsells and in particular the one to Captain Robert Maunsell who was a middy under Nelson. The Maunsell family owned Thorpe Malsor Hall for some years and were great benefactors to the village.

LODDINGTON is a small village lying a few miles from Kettering and midway between the A43 and the A6 or A14. The ironstone church of **ST LEONARD'S**, has a lovely spire and tower built, with the rest of the church during the thirteenth century. Notice the large curious moulding over the west doorway of the west tower, said by one historian to have been once used as a cover for a large statue. The doorway itself is a masterful piece of period architecture with deep moulded arches and three columns on each side. Also look for the four gargoyles along the west and east ends of the tower. The font is possibly Saxon and in the south aisle we find a piscina and an aumbrey which tells us that there was once an altar there. Look for the hour glass stand by the pulpit, unfortunately the glass has long gone, but this was used years ago to limit the length of the sermons! While in the chancel look to the south of the altar and see the beautiful stained glass window by William Morris (1834 -1896). The church leaflet tells us that the window was completed in 1893 as a memorial to the son of the Rector.

Unusual gable, Loddington

CRANSLEY, off the main Northampton to Kettering road consists of two villages, Great and Little Cransley. **ST ANDREW'S** is a very fine church the greater part being transitional from Early English to the Decorated periods of architecture, although the tower and clerestory are of a later period. Look for the lovely stained glass window in the west tower wall, put there so it faces America, for this window is dedicated to all the people who lost their lives in the Second World War and who flew planes from the local air fields, and in particular the American pilots. Also notice the unusual cranes in the medieval windows, the emblem of the Cransley family.

Built out of that lovely, warm brown Northamptonshire ironstone, **ST ANDREW'S CHURCH, BROUGHTON** is found in the village, now bypassed on the A43 Northampton to Kettering road. The church was restored in 1854 and the chancel

rebuilt in 1828, but the old work includes Norman, Decorated and Perpendicular periods. The south doorway is Norman and shows a typical arch with zigzag mouldings on. The Norman church probably had no aisles and the buttress in the south-west is probably Norman and the west window in the tower, together with bell openings and ogee arches are late thirteenth century (Early English). There is a marble bust to Harold Kynnesman, he was treasurer to Queen Elizabeth's army during the ill fated Irish rebellion and he was subsequently executed. Also find the memorial to Robert Bolton who was a well known writer at the time and rector of Bozeat from 1610 till 1631.

ORTON CHURCH is now used as a training centre for the encouragement of the traditional stonemasonry skills and courses are held here to train stonemasons. The church was acquired in 1977, and later they took over the village church of **ST PETER** in Little Oakley where more courses were held. At the time of writing the church is now being used for worship as the Orton Trust is negotiating with the company to use the church again for training. The Orton trust was founded in 1968 and in 1977 they took over St Peters, Little Oakley for monumental training and they had the honour of repairing the St Albans tomb.

Orton Church of **ALL SAINTS** has a Norman tower and later added to during the medieval period. There is also a Norman chancel arch and one in the nave. There is an interesting circular font with four faces both human and animal.

The whole of the fabric of the church has been left in its natural state since it was taken over by the trust, but gaining entrance to the church is only available when courses are in progress.

ST MARY'S CHURCH, BURTON LATIMER, although originally a Norman cruciform church, has been heavily restored, especially during the nineteenth century. There are still several interesting features to explore and see. The south arcade has two Norman arches. There are also Norman circular piers and square capitals with scallops. The north arcade with half an arch follows early in the thirteenth century. There is also further early thirteenth century work with pointed arches around the church, and the south doorway. The tower was rebuilt in 1866 but the battlements and spire are of the fourteenth century and although the east window is around 1867 the side windows are thirteenth century. The north door through which you enter has two large double doors, studded with nails and the date 1500 on. Several remnants of medieval and Elizabethan wall paintings are worth seeing. St Catherine on the north aisle wall is from the fourteenth century, and near the west end the martyrdom of a saint. Further Elizabethan paintings are found around the walls. A monument to the Boyvill family (early sixteenth century), sadly vandalised, so that all that remains now is their group of children. Other brass monuments remember some of the members of the Lords of the Manor.

WARKTON CHURCH dedicated to **ST EDMUND** has a magnificent Perpendicular tower rising through four stages to seventy feet. The church was incorporated as part of an estate planned by Ralph Montagu during the seventeenth century and modelled on Versailles, also including Boughton House and the village of Weekley. The nave has two Norman arches with fifteenth century clerestory windows. Further additions throughout the centuries seem to have been built to accommodate the monuments to the Montagu's and Buccleuch's. The chancel, for instance, was built after 1749 to house the memorial to 'Planter John' and later his children.

The church of **ST MARY'S, WEEKLEY** sits quietly and peacefully tucked away in the village, adjacent to one of the entrances to Boughton House and also next to the old almshouses, once the Montagu Hospital (1611), and which displays a beautiful sundial. The church was built mainly during the thirteenth to fifteenth centuries, but does include a lovely Norman south doorway. Like Warkton church St Mary's has many tombs to the Montagu's, who also used this church for their services and were responsible for much of its upkeep and restoration. The south chapel appears to be the main one for the Montagus and there is a superb alabaster painted ceremonial figure of Sir Edward Montagu, the Chief Justice who died in 1557. Close by is the canopied tomb of the second Sir Edward (1601) and his wife Elizabeth. Explore and look for further memorials around the church.

The church of **ST JAMES, GRAFTON UNDERWOOD** has stood on this site for over 800 years and is a mixture of architectural periods with the oldest parts of the late

Norman period to be found in the tower and nave. The original building probably had a steep roof, commencing from the lower side walls and it was this with the steeple that was probably early Norman, together with the clerestory windows. Look for the small leper's squint in the corner of the east end of the south wall, this enabled lepers to follow the communion service, and an unusual gargoyle on the left of the altar of a boy with praying hands. He is thought to be a stonemason's apprentice, aged about 14 years. Over the arch are gargoyles of the miller and his wife.

The memorial south window depicting a flying fortress bomber and badges of the support groups from the local airfield is dedicated to 1579 members of the American Eighth Air Force who gave their lives whilst serving at Grafton Underwood airfield during World War II and especially members of the 384 Bombardment Group. Sited up on the Geddington Road where you will find a magnificent granite memorial at the end of number one runway. A photograph of the window hangs in the main entrance of the Pentagon in Washington and a replica window is in the Chapel of the museum in Utah USA.

Murals on the north walls are too bad to be restored, but there are traces of the Lords Prayer and the Ten Commandments and in the churchyard you will find a Celtic Cross - a memorial to Lord Castleton (Vernon), who died in 1883 and the vault is entered by steps and contains eight coffins, the last funeral being in 1937.

ALL SAINTS, WILBARSTON, together with the village nestle in the Welland Valley, once part of Rockingham Forest and the Rockingham Estate and offer magnificent views over the Welland Valley. The church has a thirteenth century spire rising out of a Norman tower. The blocked in priest's door and carvings on the capitals at each end of the north arcade are also Norman. It is also thought that the round plain font may be as old as the church. All Saints has a wonderfully painted ceiling and charming oak screen.

The village of **ASHLEY** is situated adjacent to the river Welland and west of Corby. The church which occupies a prominent position on the north side of the village is dedicated to **ST MARY THE VIRGIN**. St Mary's, dating from about 1300 was rebuilt, with the exception of the west tower, in ironstone and grey limestone in the Decorated style by Sir GG Scott in 1867. The reredos in the church is of alabaster. Look for the beautiful pink marble font and the elaborate brass chancel gates adorned on the top with lilies. The result of the interior is of great opulence as no expense was spared.

ST MARY'S CHURCH, WESTON BY WELLAND was first built during the thirteenth century and entirely rebuilt along the same plan in 1866, and at the expense of the local landowners and the Rev Samuel Danby, the vicar. If your eyes will allow you, look for the carved heads on the battlements of the tower.

ST MARY'S CHURCH, SUTTON BASSETT is separated from Leicestershire by the River Welland and is small in comparison to most of our county churches, with a nave, chancel and an attractive bellcote. St Mary's is basically a Norman building with a Norman window in the north wall of the chancel, a Norman doorway in the nave and two round arches on massive columns separating the nave from a narrow south aisle. Additionally there are beautiful Norman carvings on the capitals of the chancel arch with further medieval stone heads supporting the wallposts in the nave roof. A picturesque church, worth visiting for its Norman characteristics.

The quaint village of **DINGLEY**, just off the A427 from Brampton Ash has a delightful churchyard surrounded by a magnificent yew hedge, with the church of **ALL SAINTS** almost entirely of the Perpendicular period. The church has a fifteenth century tower and Norman arcades on the south aisle of the nave and chancel. The south porch is almost six hundred years old - look for the carved angel in prayer in the roof. Many memorials are to the Hungerford family who lived in Dingley Hall during the nineteenth century. Two monuments remember the 8th and 9th Viscount Downe - two famous soldiers, but there is also a memorial to the wife of Admiral Beatty, the great sailor of First World War fame, who owned the Hall for a while, and Ethel his wife died here in 1932. Her brass shows her kneeling at a prayer desk..

ST MARY'S CHURCH, BRAMPTON ASH sits alongside the A427 on high ground and offering a spectacular view of the adjoining fields of rich pasture land. The church is in the early Perpendicular style and has a magnificent broach spire and an Early English chancel. There is a fine headless brass of a fifthteenth century knight in armour, reputed to be of Sir John Holt and also one of Simon de Norwich bare headed with his wife Isabel and their dog. According to tradition it was one of the Norwich family who, early in the eighteenth century, lost the whole lordship "at one throw of the dice" to Sarah Duchess of Marlborough, through whose second daughter is descended to the Spencers of Althorp.

Look around the tower to find bands of carved animals. What can you spot? Lions, monsters? Also look closely to find water spouts around the church all with carved faces and animals and the bricked up priest's door.

ST BOTOLPH'S CHURCH, STOKE ALBANY is mainly thirteenth century and in a delightful setting by the village green. Over the porch is a sundial and an interesting wooden board which demands that men scrape their shoes and women take off their pattens before entering church - a sign that we did not always have good tarmac paths and roads!! Also in the porch is a great curiosity - a monumental tablet with this inscription:

> *Here lyeth ye body of Francis Parker who gave to ye pore of this parish*
> *ten shillings a yeare to be paid of Lamas day every yeare.*
> *For ever, upon this grave stone. February ye 4th, 1683".*

On the stone seat beneath are holes in which the coins were placed. On the south wall is a tablet to Lord Denman who died in this parish in 1854, and is buried in the churchyard close to the North wall of the chancel, where, on his tombstone, it is recorded that "by giving two extra years of sittings he rendered delays almost impossible in all our courts". He was Chief Justice Denman, and also Solicitor-General, born in 1779 and, during the years he was Chief Justice he sat on many trials. He defended Queen Caroline, speaking for ten hours in her defence, persuading Parliament to withdraw the Divorce Bill. Later in his life he also made speeches for the freedom of slavery. Interestingly the researcher's mother's maiden name was Denham!!

The church of **ST GILES, DESBOROUGH** is mainly Early English architecture and is a very fine building, occupying a commanding position and having a good pinnacled tower and spire. The interior is very imposing with mural monuments to the Pulton family who were Lord's of the Manor for over thirteen generations. Like many churches over the ages the spire was struck by lightning on the 9 August 1843 but was soon restored by the parishioners. Over the centuries several Saxon remains have been found around the church and rectory, many of which are in the British Museum, but also giving rise to a strong possibility that there was a Saxon church on the site. Three large stones, one with Saxon scrollwork, a crude picture possibly representing Daniel in the lion's den have been found together with a Saxon grave unearthing a necklace and gold cross pendant.

ROTHWELL is an attractive old shoemaking town and best known for its large open market square, with several old appealing buildings - the market house, hospital and church - all having been dominant over the years. **HOLY TRINITY** church, notable for its size and brightness, is the longest in the county (173 feet) and was once possibly larger. The blocked arches on the outer walls of the north and south sides of the church show that the transepts once extended out into the churchyard. The arcading at the top of the wall by the Ragsdale Tomb, in the south-east aisle, continue through to the outside, suggesting that possibly this south transept continued further east.

The church, built of local ironstone, had its beginnings during William the Conqueror's reign and five Norman windows are still seen above the arcading on the south of the chancel. Entering the chancel notice the rood screen stairs and the ancient medieval carved choir stalls on either side. The misericords are carved with angels, a dragon and kings. Beyond the choir stalls and on the north side of the chancel a fragment of a reddish-brown wall painting is visible on the underside of the arch. At the furthest point in the chancel there are four thirteenth century stone priests seats (an unusual number), and opposite is the 'William de Rothwell' brass. William held an important position from Edward Ill.

Retrace your steps to the eastern end of the south transept and find the Owen Ragsdale brass and altar tomb. This commemorates the man responsible for building Jesus Hospital, found off the Market Square and near to the church. Look for the pelican emblem on the inside of his tomb. This same pelican appears again on the south side of the Market House and in the courtyard of the Hospital. Although there are many interesting points in the church to look for and find, a visit to the bone crypt, entered through the south door, is essential for the explorer. It was in about 1700 that a gravedigger discovered the charnel house and the remains of about 1500 persons. Are the bones those of the Danish invaders, victims from the Battle of Naseby or of sufferers of the Black Death? We may never know, but, nevertheless, an interesting find and a must for the visitor to see.

Leaving the church, return to the Market Place along the path with the graveyard on your right. Immediately on leaving the path, and to the right, is the Hospital. Built in the late sixteenth century, Ragsdale on his death left instructions that the twenty-five places should be offered to the poor. Walk through the elegant doorway into the peace of the courtyard to see this Elizabethan almshouse.

Originally **RUSHTON** had two churches, St Peter's sited on the Rushton Hall estate, which was bought by William Tresham in 1437 and the church doubled up as the private chapel to the manor and as the parish church. Additionally, Rushton is mentioned in the Domesday Book as having two villages - Rushton All Hallows and Rushton St Peter's. However the former was considered to have a greater population and therefore more important and in 1780 the two parishes became one and in 1799 the estate church was ordered to be demolished.

ALL SAINTS with its beautiful Northamptonshire ironstone has a Norman nave with thirteenth century arches dividing it from the north aisle and later to fifteenth century windows. Find in this area the detailed marble figure of William de Goldingham, a knight who was laid to rest in 1296. The figure is supposed to show one of the most complete examples of chain armour in the country! Between the chapel and the chancel is the altar tomb of Sir Thomas Tresham, grandfather of the builder, who died in 1559 and his tomb was removed from St Peter's Church when it was demolished. Again this tomb is unique as he was the last English Grand Prior of the Knights Hospitallers and there is no other tomb in the country showing a Grand Prior wearing his robes of office. Two rarities worth spending time admiring. Finally stop to admire the three fifteenth century stone priest seats with their richly carved canopies of men and animals.

PIPEWELL, once the site of a Cisercian monastery founded in the twelfth century but sadly nothing now remains - several items from the Abbey have found their way into local churches - the medieval screen at Brigstock and stalls at Great Oakley. The church of **ST MARY**, possibly lying close to the abbey site was erected in 1881.

NEWTON IN THE WILLOWS, lies snugly in the tranquil countryside well away from the rushing traffic

and we find the church dedicated to **ST FAITH** sitting in the fields away from the village itself. Now redundant but restored into a local authority field study centre, St Faith's was once the private chapel incorporated within the Tresham family home with a Huge dovecote nearby. Now only the church and dovecote remain.

Many of the furnishings and memorials have been removed to churches nearby but once there were many memorials to the Tresham family dating back to 1400. Included in the church was a brass to John Mulsho and his wife Joan Tresham with the figure of St Faith holding the grid on which she was martyred. The brass is now in Geddington Church. Historians consider that there was once an old barn with the relics of a second church built into its walls.

ST MARY MAGDALENE is situated in a beautiful picturesque setting with the Queen Eleanor Cross dominating the centre of the village, and at the junction of three roads. Geddington Church is a few yards from the square, which is surrounded by old cottages, many of which are thatched. Although **GEDDINGTON** is mentioned in the Domesday Book there is evidence of an early Saxon church in the village. This evidence can be seen in the north aisle of the church. Look above the rounded Norman windows of the north aisle and find the line of arcading which suggests that a church was in existence before the Norman conquest (1066), and during the Saxon period. The arcading, which the Saxons used to adorn the out-

side of their churches was probably the former outer wall of the church when the church consisted of only the nave. Notice also the line of the steep pitched roof over the chancel arch. The north was added in the twelfth century. An interesting recent addition in the north aisle is the alabaster slab depicting Robert Tresham and his wife, Isabel, and the floor brass, a memorial to John Mulsho and his wife Joan Tresham. Both the slab and the brass were brought to Geddington from St Faith's Church at Newton-in-the-Willows when this church was closed and became a field study centre. In the same aisle is a brass with a portrait of the wife of Thomas Tresham, and above this the Tresham arms, with the Tresham Screen at the eastern end of the south aisle, shows the arms and initials with the date 1618.

Interestingly, in 1290 the body of Queen Eleanor rested overnight in the Castle Chapel on her journey to Westminster Abbey where she was buried on 17 December 1290. Apart from fragments of stone nothing remains of the church, although the Eleanor Cross erected in 1294 stands as her memorial.

The 179 foot perpendicular spire of **ST PETER AND ST PAUL, KETTERING,** dating around 1450 dominates the old town around the Market Place, Sheep Street, the Tourist Centre and the Alfred East Gallery.

The church is in the later style of English architecture, consisting of a nave and side aisles, a chancel, north and south chantry, and the lofty tower and spire of equal heights, about 88 feet each. The tower consists of three storeys, ornamented with double buttresses and octagonal turrets at the angles, and surmounted by a handsome hexagonal crocketed spire with three windows. Around the base is an embattled parapet, connected with the angular turrets. It is very noticeable that the tower and porch are not in line with other parts of the building; the former inclines somewhat to the north and the porch to the west to make the approach more direct from the market place. Entering the church gives a calm, quiet atmosphere away from the bustling streets outside. Look for the remains of a painting of St James the Greater on the wall of the north aisle. It is now hardly recognisable.

In the south chapel, called "Sawyers Aisle," are the stairs and doorway leading to the rood loft. The Sawyer family were prominent in Kettering during the seventeenth century and a legacy left by Edmund Sawyer built the original hospital in 1688, now the old Almshouses for you to see in Sheep Street

The church of **ST BOTOLPH, BARTON SEAGRAVE** is an impressive example of Norman architecture, with a beautiful north Norman doorway. Further examples of Norman architecture are all around the church - the superb broad arches in the lower tower, the windows in the tower and chancel, a lovely Norman tympanum in the north doorway and a Norman font.

Two interesting memorials must be found - one to John Bridges, the historian who died in 1724 and who has a long Latin inscription, and the brass to Jane Floyd, wife of a rector, and wearing a huge ruff and hood who sadly died in 1616 leaving a baby and two older children, all three pictured in the brass. The husband in his grief adds the inscription to the brass:

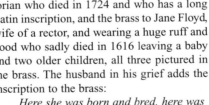

> *Here she was born and bred, here was
> she married,
> Here did she live and die, thus was she
> buried.
> This brass can say no more.*

The church of **ST PETER** in **DEENE** was originally built during the twelfth century and extensively restored and enlarged in 1868 by Lady Adeline Cardigan in memory of her husband James, the 7th Earl of Cardigan, who was famous for his role in the Battle of Balaclava and the Charge of the Light Brigade.

The south chapel remains a shrine of monuments to the Brudenall family who have lived in Northamptonshire since the thirteenth century and

owned Deene Park since 1514. The monuments start around 1531 progressing through the years to include the beautiful carved white marble table tomb of the 7th Earl of Cardigan.

There is much to see and admire in St Peter's, which is now preserved by the British Heritage.

Above: South doorway, Deene

ST NICHOLAS' CHURCH, BULWICK with its tall and impressive Perpendicular tower is one of the few churches in the county with flying buttresses supporting the tower, and as you enter the church there is a beautiful welcoming poem inside the door. The chancel is late thirteenth century as are the sedilia and piscina. The magnificent Bulwick Hall was built in the seventeenth century for the Tryon family and many memorials around the church depict sad events and tales. One memorial chronicles the death of Admiral Tryon who perished in HMS Victoria when it was accidentally rammed by HMS Camperdown in the Mediterranean in 1893. A John Thomas Tryon was rector of the parish, others including five males were killed in the First World War and a Henry Tryon aged 25 died commanding a night attack on Sebastopol. Sad memorials but all telling a story.

As we looked around the outside of **ALL SAINTS, LAXTON** we were taken aback by the wonderful gargoyle water spouts around the roof - possibly designed and carved by Lord Carbery during the 1860's when he was also responsible for restoring the church. Look for the Norman spiral designs on the capitals of the south doorway - these are probably the oldest stone in the church. Several memorials to the Carbery's are found in the church.

ST JAMES' GRETTON began as an aisleless church in Norman times and then in 1130 the west aisle and north aisle were added. In the thirteenth century both aisles were extended and the east aisle and new chancel were added. Interesting relics include the fifteenth century font, Georgian box pews and wall memorial tablets to the Hatton family who used to own Kirby Hall.

GREAT OAKLEY is close to becoming a suburb of Corby, but once in the village and close to the park with Harpers Brook flowing nearby your thoughts soon drift away from suburbia Corby.

ST MICHAEL'S CHURCH is situated in the grounds of the Tudor Hall, once possibly adjoining the church, and the keys, if you are lucky, are obtained from the Estate office. With no one about when we visited we had to be content to look through the windows! The wonderful nave roof built with Collyweston slates is pitched down to the eaves of the chancel with the low battlemented Norman tower and windows. Inside there are stalls from the old Pipewell Abbey with marvellous misericords with the most lovely carvings of a swan with its family, an angel and Father Time with his scythe and hourglass. On the poppyheads are saints with heads of men and lions at the sides. Look for the figured tiles in the chancel, they also came from nearby Pipewell Abbey. There are several interesting monumental inscriptions commemorating members of the Brooke family; who have owned Great Oakley Hall for over five centuries. The earliest appears to be a brass tablet in the south wall to the memory of

Thomas Brooke, Esq.(1557), the builder of the present mansion. Sir Arthur de Capell Brooke helped to found the Royal Geographical Society.

There are many artefacts to look for and admire in the church - the two family pews, one of which forms part of the vestry, a chest tomb dated 1660, tantony and a sanctus bell, both extremely old and a plaque in memory of Peter Dent one of the longest serving priests associated with the church.

ST PETER'S CHURCH and the village of **LITTLE OAKLEY** were once in a clearing deep in Rockingham Forest and in the north aisle is a lifesize stone figure of a forester carved as if he were lying in a coffin. He carries a cross-bow and wears a short kirtle. The thirteenth century church has been added to and restored over the years and has a tower with a small pyramid style cap. The Montagus used to live in the manor house and there is a memorial to William Montagu (1619), in the church. The church was once a part of the "Orton Trust". A trust founded in 1968 with the aim of encouraging the traditional stonemasonry skills used in the restoration and conservation of historic buildings. Its activities are based on the redundant church at Orton. In 1977 the trust acquired St. Peter's which was then leased to a company specialising in monument restoration. The trust arranges monthly, residential week-end courses in stonemasonry skills. When we first visited the church the company in residence were repairing the St Albans tomb, and they had tables all laid out down the main aisle with the pieces of the tomb, it looked like a giant jig-saw puzzle.

ST MARY MAGDALENE, built of ironstone is situated at the south end of **COTTINGHAM** village and was built mainly during the thirteenth to fifteenth centuries, although the tower is thirteenth and fourteenth century with a well preserved Norman window above the arch. Look at the capitals of the arcades to find unique carvings. On one capital four figures are lying round head to head, Mary Magdalene, the Abbot of Peterborough and the Lords of Cottingham and the neighbouring village; symbolising the authority of the church, the parish and the two manors. Another capital has a dwarf and a mythical creature, and a further one two unknown ladies lying head to head. Fascinating to think that these are around 700 years old!

EAST CARLTON lies just outside Corby on the Market Harborough road. The church dedicated to **ST PETER** was rebuilt in 1708. The south chapel contains several monuments to the Palmer family, dating from 1670.The monument of 1673 to Sir Geoffrey Palmer and his wife consists of two upright figures made of alabaster wrapped in their shrouds encased in black marble and having hair styles of Charles II period. There is a double tier pulpit and box pews. The tower has a beautiful frieze carved below the parapet and four pinnacles with weather vanes at each corner.

The church dedicated to **ST JOHN THE BAPTIST in OLD CORBY** stands proudly on the main A427 road from the Weldon roundabout on the A43. Interestingly this church has been re-dedicated, originally being dedicated to St Peter and dating from the late twelfth or early thirteenth century.

Like many of our churches St Peter's has been developed over the years and whilst the upper section of the spire was added in 1350, sadly it came crashing down through the nave when struck by lightning in 1801. It was several years later before funds became available to repair and rebuild the nave and spire. In 1625 a new south door was built but the outline of the old one can still be seen above the inner door of the porch. Look for the sundial added above the outer door inscribed 'JP 1625 - John Parker being the benefactor.

Just inside the door on the left against the wall is a tomb recently found when they took up an old carpet. The church pamphlet tells us that it is the tomb of John Lee dated 1652. Interestingly it has a rhyming inscription which reads:

> "Here lyeth the body of John Lee
> Who departed at age about sixty three,
> And though his body here confined be,
> his name live to perpetuity.
> And when it is time then from the dust,
> shall live with ye soul with the just."

Above the words, a skull and bones are depicted, with the name ELIZABETH LEE, wife of the deceased.

The Lady Chapel in the north aisle was dedicated in 1969. Look in the chancel on the south wall above the choir stalls for there you can see an eroded Green Man. Outside just right of the porch entry, low down we found a scratch dial. In the churchyard almost facing the porch is an early chest tomb which has badly eroded shields it is reputed to be that of John Neville, Lord Latimer of 1488. His family were Lords of the Manor of Corby for nearly 350 years.

ST JOHN THE BAPTIST, WAKERLEY is basically late Norman with a beautiful chancel arch of that period, which also has a double band of chevrons and carved capitals, one showing knights in armour laying siege to a castle. Explore around the church and you will find more Norman work. During the next three centuries further building and alterations took place, including a fifteenth century tower and spire, a superb roof with wallposts resting on carved stone corbels and coloured busts and figures on the main roof beams. The two transept chapels, built on either side of the nave were also added, showing splendid arches and above the south one are the remains of a Norman arch. There is a monument to Richard Cecil (1633), the son of Lord Burghley. Richard built himself a large mansion nearby to the church. The church is now only used for two services a year, All Saints Day and Harvest Festival and is cared for by the Redundant Churches Scheme.

The two villages **GREAT AND LITTLE WELDON** or as its old name was, Weldon-in-the-Woods, allows you to romanticise and imagine in olden times that the church, situated in a clearing in Rockingham Forest would have the tower lantern lit in the evening, acting as a beacon to help the travellers and workers in the forest find their way to the sanctuary of the village for the night. Tradition has it that one such traveller lost in the forest, made his way to safety by seeing the church, and who afterwards financed the building of the domed lantern as a thank-offering. The lantern still continues to be lit on New Year's Eve.

ST MARY'S is chiefly Early English architecture with additions over the next few centuries, although there is a Norman tower arch with a carved head.

The church has wonderful stained glass, the youngest, so to speak, is the memorial window to the USAAF 401st Bombardment group in memory of the airmen of the Deenthorpe airbase who lost their lives in the Second World War (1939-1945). Also look for the wonderful and weird array of gargoyles around the exterior walls of the aisles.

The surrounding countryside is dominated by the Perpendicular (fifteenth century) spire of **ST PETER'S CHURCH, STANION**, having a commanding position on a hill above the valley of the River Nene. Inside the church around the south aisle there is a fantastic corbel decoration with around fifty heads offering every kind of look - the sequence broken by a giant gargoyle with a water-spout in its mouth. There is also a wall painting of a stag, unicorn and a cowled figure - research into this found no reference other than it was probably fifteenth century. Mystery paintings!. The highly decorated font is also fifteenth century.

A very interesting tale comes to light when you see the giant rib from a cow, (known as the Dun Cow Rib). The gigantic cow owned by the villagers grazed in the meadow close to the village and she knew all the villagers. When they came to her she filled their jugs and containers and when these were full she stopped, making sure there was enough milk for all the village people. A coven of witches heard about the cow and they became very jealous and sent one of their sisters to get rid of the cow. The witch came with a sieve and sat by the cow and the cow tried to fill the sieve but naturally could not. She collapsed and died. The villagers were very sad and to keep the witches away they had a rib cut out of the cow which was consecrated in the church. The poor old cow was buried in a field adjacent to the Corby road and which became known as "Cowthick".

ROCKINGHAM village dominated by the castle straddles the A6116 as it stretches down into the Welland Valley. The church, which is only open when the castle and grounds are open is dedicated to **ST LEONARD**, the Patron Saint of Prisoners, and stands just below the north courtyard of the castle.

The church suffered severely during the Civil War, the tower and most of the church was destroyed by Cromwell's forces. The tower was re-erected and new windows of the late Decorated style and character supplied. The chancel was restored during the mid-nineteenth century and a memorial chapel added for the Watson family, who leased the Castle from Henry VIII in 1530 and bought the freehold in 1619. The Watson's have lived there continuously from 1619 apart from a brief period during the Civil War when it was occupied by the Roundheads. Over subsequent years the Watson's have been responsible for major repairs and restoration of the church. Naturally there are many interesting monuments to the family in the church.

HARRINGWORTH village is dominated by the fantastic viaduct straddling the Welland Valley and which used to carry the old London Midland Scottish railway from Kettering to Oakham. This wonderful feat of engineering, built in 1874-79 has 82 arches spanning the valley for nearly a mile, each arch being over 40 feet wide; but now alas it is only used for freight traffic.

The church, dedicated to **ST JOHN THE BAPTIST** is full of memorials to the Tryons, including a crypt to the family, which is cut off from the nave and north aisle by spiked railings.

The twelfth century tower has a spire added two centuries later and at its base are carved heads, one sticking out its tongue.

Before leaving the church admire the magnificent kneelers at the altar rail which stretch across the chancel; they are a pictorial record of the Harringworth Viaduct and the plaque to Rector Matthew Palmer, 1752, who died at the age of 110.

Arthur Mee in Northamptonshire says that the sanctus bell was rung daily when Joan of Arc was driving our soldiers out of France, another bell was rung at the coming of the Stuarts with the Coronation of James the First.

Before leaving look for the coffin in the churchyard which has been hewn out of block stone. This was found in 1932 about three feet below the surface in a field on the left hand side of the road to Laxton at the top of the hill known as Scotgate. The coffin laying north-south is believed to date from the Roman occupation. A similar coffin was found a year later but was too badly damaged to be removed to the churchyard.

Visiting the **COLLYWESTON** church on a lovely spring morning suggested elegance and beauty in a church so lovingly cared for by the parishioners. The pews and choir stalls had been profusely polished and were showing off their carved poppyheads and pelicans; symbolising a Christian sacrifice. All were a joy to see.

Dedicated to **ST ANDREW** the church was built by Ralph Cromwell in about 1440 possibly as a thanksgiving for his safe return from the Battle of Agincourt, where he fought with his brothers.

There are Saxon origins in the south wall of the chancel and this can be seen by the small window. The crocketed pinnacles of the west tower are from the sixteenth century and the arch of the south doorway, which possibly came from the manor house, is surrounded by a moulding of carved flowers. Lady Margaret Beaufort, mother of Henry VII lived in the manor house as did Ralph Cromwell. It is worth finding the dovecote on the site of the old manor house to see the inscription 'ER 1570'.

A beautiful stained glass window in the south aisle is dedicated to 2nd Lt Colins Close of the Northamptonshire Regiment, killed in battle in the 1914-18 war and the large south annexe known as the Tryon chapel, lay sad and empty on our visit. The sad story of Admiral Tryon is related in our visit to Bulwick church.

ALL SAINTS AND ST JAMES, KINGS CLIFFE is one of the cruciform style churches - the Norman central tower, with its thirteenth century spire allowing the aisles to lead out from the middle to the chapels and to form the crucifix. The tower walls have a variety of gargoyles and faces staring at you.

Look for the lovely carved bench ends which came from the Fotheringhay collegiate when the choir was pulled down in 1548. Look also around the stained glass and find the angels with musical instruments, it is thought that these also came from Fotheringhay and there are also fragments of glass from Barnack Manor. The four-teenth century font has unique carvings showing the emblems of the four evangelists together with a lily, a rose, a vine and a landscape with trees, rocks and a river.

Find the unusual tomb in the churchyard of Willam Law. It is in the form of a writing desk and is near the north transept. William Law, born in the village in 1686 was an important theologian and also fellow of Emmanual College, Cambridge but he had to resign his Fellowship as it meant taking the Oath of Allegiance to George I. He returned to Kings Cliffe and died there in 1761. His library in Bridge Street, Kings Cliffe contains many of his books. A royal residence or hunting lodge known as "Kings House" once stood on the south side of the churchyard.

The village is a wonderful place to spend time exploring with its Collyweston slated roofs, you might think you were in the Cotswolds.

DUDDINGTON, sitting adjacent to the River Welland, with its Cotswold characteristics due to the local Collyweston slate, is one of the most attractive villages in Northamptonshire.

The parish church of **ST MARY'S** is situated in the centre of the village and is particularly noted for its unusual south position of the tower, possibly due to the falling ground down to the river on the west side.

Most of the church is of the Early English period although the tower still sits on its Norman base with a small Norman doorway leading into the tower, and there are also six Norman arches in the nave. Look at the pan-elling on the box pews and the monuments to the Jackson family who still live in the manor.

There is much to see and admire in the church and village of Duddington including the fourteenth century medieval bridge.

What a fantastic view greeted us as we went through the churchyard gate that gorgeous warm and sunny February afternoon. There to greet us was a magnificent carpet of snowdrops all the way up to the church door. Approaching the church door look up to see gargoyle faces looking down on you from the church tower.

ALL SAINTS CHURCH, EASTON ON THE HILL dating from around the twelfth century has been developed and enjoyed over the centuries and stands at the north end of the village and is set high on the hill.

When paying for a leaflet about the church, money is put into the mouth of a fifteenth century gargoyle, which originally fell off the tower when it was struck by lightning in 1915.

As you walk down the nave look up on your right to see the remnants of a window of the church that was on this sight before the present one. The church is very light and airy due to the total lack of stained glass. Look for the poppyheads on the end of the choir stalls. The church still retains it's old oak pews and there are quite a few box pews, some with the names of the families who used them. Look for the tablet to the memory of Lancellott Skynner - the Rector's son who was lost at sea when the La Lutine was wrecked off the coast of Holland in 1791. The ship's bell was recovered and is now the famous bell which hangs at Lloyds in the City of London.

The view from the top of the tower is extensive and beautiful. Boston church and Ely cathedral, a distance of about 32 miles being visible on a good clear day. The town of Stamford can also be seen from the church-yard. The tower of this church was used as a station by the ordnance surveyors in 1843.

Just to the west of the church stands the Priest's house, (now looked after by the National Trust). It was at one time a stable, but was restored into a meeting house and museum.

BLATHERWYCKE church is dedicated to **THE HOLY TRINITY** and has a wonderful tomb to the poet Thomas Randolph, who died in 1635 at the age of 29, whilst on a visit to the village. The tablet was carved by Nicholas Stone and is written in delightful Elizabethan English and is worth reproducing :

> Here sleepe thirteene together in one tombe
> And all these greate, yet quarrell not for roome.
> The Muses and ye Graces teares did meete.
> And grav'd these letters on ye churlish sheete;
> Who having wept, their fountaines drye,
> Through the Conduit of the eye,
> For their freind who here does lye,
> Crept into his grave and dyed,
> And soe the riddle is untyed,
> For which this church, proud that the Fates bequeath
> Unto her ever-honour'd trust,
> Soe much and that soe precious dust,
> Hath crown'd her Temples with an Ivye wreath;
> Which should have Laurell been,
> But yt the greived Plant to se him dead
> Tooke pet and withered.

Another wall monument is to one Thomas Cole who in 1864 left money to buy six of the oldest poor gentlemen of the village a plum pudding every Christmas day.

Sir Humphrey Stafford built the Elizabethan Hall and there are many monuments to the family around the church. Perhaps the most delightful one is to Sir Humphrey himself. He died in 1548 and his wall monument has two classical columns showing the Stafford knot, with carved panels including Sir Humphrey's wife, sons and daughters.. The church has a lovely Norman tower and a blocked Norman south doorway.

The Nene Valley

The Nene Valley is one of the dominant features of the county, owing its appearance to the last Ice Age, when the melting water chopped off the hills. Rising at Badby the River Nene flows off the Northamptonshire Heights forming a natural geographical location for many towns and villages. Northampton, Wellingborough, Thrapston and Oundle all lie close to the flood plain of the river. The Nene's rich arable and pasture lands, combined with a navigable river encouraged the early settlers to make their homes, resulting in some of the oldest settlements and churches in the county. Wherever you look the Nene Valley landscape will be dotted with spires and towers of the village churches.

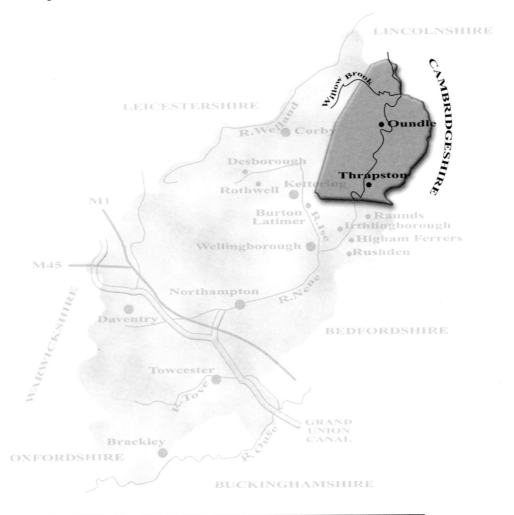

ALL SAINTS, SUDBOROUGH is largely built during the thirteenth and fourteenth centuries with a great deal of restoration during the nineteenth century. The cross-legged figure under an arch in the north wall of the chancel represents Sir Robert de Vere, standard bearer to William Longsword, the son of the Earl of Salisbury. The son lead a Crusade in 1249 and here you see the memorial to the knight and standard bearer. His crossed legs are symbolic of death whilst fighting in the Crusades.

At the east end of the north aisle are figures in brass to the West family, one of whom is described as a "Marbler" signifying that he was a carver of marble figures, etc. Look for the decorated buttresses in the chancel and the very ornate sedilia.

CRANFORD ST JOHN AND CRANFORD ST ANDREW are two separate but closely united villages with each having its own church. Both churches are of late Norman built during the twelfth century, but sadly **ST ANDREW'S**, below, church is now closed, although access can be gained through telephoning a number available from the Kettering TIC.

Both churches have Flemish influence. Look for the seventeenth century biblical scenes in the east chapel window of St Andrew's and the pulpit in **ST JOHN'S**, left, showing the carved figure of Pilate washing his hands and the High Priest tearing his raiment.

The pulpit in St Andrew's also has carved panels depicting the disciples - here Christ is washing his disciples feet and there are scenes of the Last Supper and Betrayal.

The east window dating from 1547 is a patchwork of several medallions and pictures with French writing. The font is medieval.

There are brasses to the Fossbroke family, right, dated 1418, these have been mounted on the wall of the north aisle. Maud Fossbroke was nurse to Henry VI. There are also wall monuments to the Robinson family who were Lords of the Manor of Cranford Hall which still stands close to the church.

The church of St John has a Norman west arch in the north arcade and conjecture surrounds the possibility that this arch has been reused and taken from somewhere else in the church as it does not quite fit in its current position. The design in the east window commemorates the union of the two parishes.

Below: Carved bench end, St Andrew's

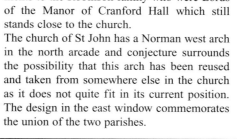

ST NICHOLAS' CHURCH, TWYWELL has many Norman features including a splendid north doorway, Norman windows, font and tower arch. Originally built on the site of an older building the stone work includes vast quantities of Northamptonshire ironstone, which for many years was quarried locally.

Two historical tales are worth recounting. The first, the nineteenth century rector, Horace Waller who was a founder member of the University Mission to Central Africa and a friend of Livingstone and General Gordon. When Livingstone died in 1873 his servants Chuma and Susi carried him 800 miles to the coast so that he could be transported back to England for burial in Westminster Abbey. The two servants were with Livingstone at the famous meeting with Stanley, they had also kept all the missionary's papers and eventually Susi and Chuma arrived with these papers at Twywell Rectory. They helped Horace Waller edit Livingstone's diaries and unfold the historical story. The second concerns Hester Mulso born in 1727 in the Elizabethan Manor House. She was a child genius and her literary writings were published by Dr Johnson in The Rambler. Her essays were widely read and she met many well known people including the King and Queen.

There is much to see and explore in St Nicholas' church. Be sure to admire the choir stalls and their carvings, African animals and scenes of slavery, and also the glass case with the memorabilia of the story of David.

SLIPTON has a small church with a nave, chancel and small bell-cote dedicated to **ST JOHN THE BAPTIST**, left. The church dating mainly from the thirteenth century has a Norman north window.

Close to the River Nene, **YARWELL** is a picturesque village in the far north of the county. **ST MARY MAGDALENE** with its pyramid tower was built during the thirteenth century and remodelled during the eighteenth. In the north chapel is the table tomb to Sir Humphrey Bellamy, a London merchant who died in 1715. The local story is that Sir Humphrey as a boy was on his way to London to join his uncle and hopefully to make his fortune. He was taken ill and recovered with care from the people of Yarwell. Sir Humphrey did make his fortune and when he died he was taken back to Yarwell to be buried and he left money to provide bread for the poor.

NASSINGTON church dedicated to **ALL SAINTS**, right, is renowned for its vastness and lofty interior. There are medieval paintings on the walls which are sadly very faded. Over the chancel arch is The Last Judgement and in the north arcade there are figures and scenes possibly of St Michael, St Catherine and St George. Also in the north aisle look for the Saxon Cross shaft, this would have stood outside the church in its early days. It dates from the tenth century and suggests that there was probably a Saxon settlement here. Parts of the nave are Saxon and the west tower arch and the north doorway are Norman. Further exploration around the church uncovers a thirteenth century west doorway with its pointed arch and dog-tooth mouldings and also aisle arches and the chancel arch from this period. The font is fourteenth century. Like many village churches Nassington is steeped in over a thousand years of history and worth visiting.

Although the church of **ST JAMES, THURNING** was almost entirely rebuilt during the nineteenth century restoration there was first a church here in Norman times, and the Norman chancel arch and north arcade still survive. In addition there are still thirteenth and fourteenth century windows in the chancel and south aisle. The oak pulpit, lectern and litany desk are all of the sixteenth century and is said that they came from All Saints, Barnwell, which was pulled down in 1825.

CLOPTON, or as was known in ancient times Clapton is close to the border of Huntingdonshire and the thirteenth century church dedicated to **ST PETER** suffered the ravages of time and fire and was completely rebuilt in 1863 by Richard Armstrong. The tall west tower, prior to rebuilding in the thirteenth century style, with a saddle-back roof, was reputed to have been one of the most handsome in the county.
The upper part of the north aisle is the burial place of the Dudley family, who for many years from 1390 owned Clopton Manor.

LUDDINGTON is a quiet village, not always mentioned on maps, and has a church dating back to the thirteenth century when the tower and chancel were built. Over the years **ST MARGARET'S** has been developed and restored. The plain octagonal font is over five hundred years old, as are the gargoyles looking down on the visitor.
Look around the pews and see Tudor panels which look like folded linen, these are called 'linenfold panels'. One historian tells us that until the latter part of the eighteenth century the church was dedicated to St Andrew but has been known as the church of St Margaret of Antioch since 1791.

ALL SAINTS, POLEBROOK is an interesting church and like Tansor has developments from Norman through to Early English. The church was built between 1175 and 1250 and stands in the centre of the village. Initially the church consisted of a nave, central tower and possibly a transept and a chancel and it is in these areas that we find the Norman work. The north transept and aisle, together with the arches in the south arcade are all Norman. There are interesting characteristics to find, such as the Norman dog-tooth carvings on the west and south windows of the tower or the leaf mouldings on the capitals. The north porch is an interestingly decorated piece of mid-thirteenth century work. The pulpit added during the seventeenth century has the hour glass for use during the sermons!!

WARMINGTON village, close to the River Nene has a church dedicated to **ST MARY.** The church is one of the county's best examples of Early English (1200-1300) architecture and the impressive octagonal spire has beautiful windows (lucarnes), which project from the spire. Built entirely during this period the arches, windows and vaulted wooden roof give the church its rich uniqueness. Look for the lovely poppy-heads, the beautiful painted chancel screen and the fifteenth century pulpit.

Three roads meet at **LUTTON** and the church dedicated to **ST PETER** which consists of a chancel, nave with north and south aisles, with a south porch and west tower, has three periods of history built into the fabric. It has several fragments of Norman moulding built into the chancel arch. In the north wall of the tower is part of a Saxon cross-shaft with interlaced work. The chancel and north arcade are Early English, and the south arcade is late thirteenth century. The clerestory and tower are of the fifteenth century. Look in the north side of the chancel to find an unusual Easter Sepulchre recess. At the east end of this wall is the strange mural monument of three bearded men kneeling facing outwards. It was set up in 1633 by Jerome Apreece, in memory of Robert, William, and Robert Apreece. On the opposite wall is another mural monument (1608), with a kneeling effigy, to Adlord Apreece.

HEMINGTON is part of the area covered by the Montagu's and then the Duke of Buccleugh's estates and in the church of **ST PETER AND ST PAUL** you will find, close to the pulpit, a brass memorial of 1517 remembering Thomas Montagu and his wife. The church was rebuilt in 1666 but retained its fifteenth century tower. Several things to look for include; the Montagu arms above the west door, the carvings of a man's and horse's head on the thirteenth century font and the stalls in the chancel. These came from Fotheringhay and have intricately carved misericords - carvings include leopards, mermaids, dwarfs, owls and eagles.

FOTHERINGHAY CHURCH dedicated to **THE BLESSED VIRGIN MARY AND ALL SAINTS** and was erected on the site of a nunnery and is a magnificent array of fifteenth century architecture and really seems out of place in the surroundings of the village. The Perpendicular windows are packed tightly between the handsome flying buttresses and carved tracery, giving the impression that there is more glass than wall. This makes the church very light inside. The elegant lantern tower rises proudly out of the main tower. The church was part of a grand plan to build a college at Fotheringhay. The college was built during the first half of the fifteenth century and survived until the dissolution in 1548. A model inside the church shows the Chantry College as it probably was, including a cloister, library, dormitories, chapter house, master's lodge and kitchen. A blocked doorway in the eastern end of the south aisle would have led into the cloister. The college buildings were situated beyond the south aisle of the church.

Either side of the altar are two memorials, one to Edward, Duke of York, who was killed at Agincourt in 1415, and one to his nephew Richard Plantagenet who also met his death in battle in 1460. Both men were instigators in the building of the college and are buried in the church. It was Richard's son who was born at Fotheringhay Castle, and who later became King Richard III. Before leaving the church look to the west end and find the small wall painting of a figure.

Fotheringhay is famous for the trial and beheading of Mary Queen of Scots in the castle in 1587 and for the birth of Richard III, but sadly the castle seems to have fallen into ruins during the early seventeenth century and was pulled down in 1635. Only a large stone and inscription remain today but together with the college and magnificent church the village has made a valuable contribution to English history.

ST ANDREW'S CHURCH, COTTERSTOCK is a mixture of styles with a splendid Decorated chancel which looks towards the River Nene. St Andrew's was originally built by John Grifford, Canon of York in connection with the founding of a college chantry in 1338 and it is only the superb chancel that remains. The church was heavily restored during the 1880's. Look for the fifteenth century brass of Robert Winteringham and the font and porch with their interesting carvings.

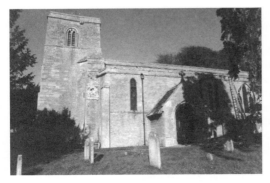

ST MARY'S, TANSOR has a complicated history. It is likely that part of the church dates from the Saxon times, but certainly there is Norman work in the current building. The main part of the nave is Norman. The round arches and two different style of piers, together with the blocked window in the west wall are all from the Norman period. The north doorway is late twelfth century. The work continued into the Early English (1200-1300) period and today we have a church with a long nave and short chancel. The church, which is lapped by the flooded Nene is also worth visiting to see the carved misericords, some of which came from Fotheringhay. Look for the carvings showing the emblem of the House of York, (Edward Duke of York was born at Fotheringhay as was King Richard III), the falcon and the fetterlock.

The church at **APETHORPE** situated in this tranquil village is dedicated to **ST LEONARD** and is mainly of the Perpendicular period. The church consists of a nave, side aisles, chancel and an embattled tower built in 1633 on which rests a pyramidal steeple. In the south aisle is the Mildmay Chapel, said to have been built around 1617 when Sir Anthony Mildmay died and to his wife Grace who died in 1620. The impressively large monument of black marble to Sir Anthony and Lady Grace Mildmay appears too large to fit in the chapel. On a massive table tomb are the recumbent effigies of Sir Anthony and Grace his wife, above them a domed canopy with alabaster curtains partly drawn. At either end the canopy is supported by huge rectangular piers, and at the four corners stand life like figures of Piety, Charity, Wisdom and Justice, while the tomb is crowned by a cupola on which is seated Charity flanked below by Faith and Hope. There is also a fine effigy to Sir Richard Dalton of 1442 - look above the head to see an unusual Annunciation scene with the figures of God, the Virgin Mary and the Archangel Gabriel.

The lovely east window in the Mildmay Chapel is in remarkably good condition for its age, with its subjects, "The Fall of Man", "The Crucifixion", "The Resurrection" and "The Last Judgement". The "Last Supper" in the chancel window is of the rare eighteenth century glass and a must to view.

Other interests in the south aisle are two helmets and enclosed in glass a tabard, worn over armour and dated around 1629. There is evidence of wall paintings and the parish is currently trying to raise funds to have them uncovered and restored.

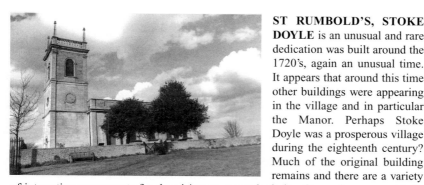

ST RUMBOLD'S, STOKE DOYLE is an unusual and rare dedication was built around the 1720's, again an unusual time. It appears that around this time other buildings were appearing in the village and in particular the Manor. Perhaps Stoke Doyle was a prosperous village during the eighteenth century? Much of the original building remains and there are a variety of interesting monuments for the visitor to see and admire. One sad monument is to the curate's wife, Hannah Roberts who died very young in 1819 and then lying beside her, her child who died a few weeks later. She lies there resting on a couch with her husband kneeling at her feet. A famous headmaster of Oundle, John Shillibeer, who was also a painter is buried here.

There is some evidence of an important Saxon Church in **OUNDLE** and the present structure of **ST PETER'S** may have been built on the site from around the thirteenth century. Below the west window in the tower a carved Saxon stone may be seen and during recent work it was discovered that the interior pillars stand on earlier footings. The tower was built during the fourteenth and fifteenth centuries and the date 1634 is visible above the southern parapet, showing the date of the rebuilding of the spire. Recent restoration has turned the Victorian stonework into a light, spacious and colourful building, also enhanced by the restoration of the Victorian reredos and medieval screens. The lectern is Flemish and the porch is from the fifteenth century. The vestry and garderobe together with the fireplace were added later, possibly to be used as a priest's dwelling. Explore the monuments and memorials in the church and as you leave admire the spire, which dominates Oundle and the surrounding countryside. A tall slender tower out of which comes a tall needle spire.

Built mainly during the thirteenth century **ST MARY AND ALL SAINTS, PILTON** stands alongside the old manor, now the rectory. The south porch is late thirteenth century although the doorway is Norman and depicts the characteristic zigzag. The church has been heavily restored over the years but it still retains thirteenth century fabric. Certain arcades and windows and the chancel arch are all from this period.

Lord Lilford, who was patron of the living and a famous ornithologist is said to have paid for the fishes, animals and birds on the pew ends and the tiles.

ST JOHN THE BAPTIST, THORPE ACHURCH situated close to Lilford Hall became the family estate of the Lilford's when St Peter's Church was demolished in 1778. Lilford Hall passed into the hands of Sir Thomas Powys in 1711 and his great grandson was made the first Lord Lilford. Sir Thomas Powys' tomb now in the south wall of the south transept was removed to St John the Baptist's after the demolition of St Peter's.

The church was originally built in the thirteenth century but was remodelled during the early 1860's. Naturally parts of the old building remain. The thirteenth century tower with its protruding windows (lucarnes) and the west doorway, windows and arches are also from the original building. Look for further monuments to the Powys family (Lord Lilford). The east window with its picture of the Good Shepherd is a memorial to the Fourth Lord Lilford who was a famous ornithologist.

TITCHMARSH CHURCH dedicated to **ST MARY** has a splendid Perpendicular (!370-1550), tower built of Weldon stone and which dominates the ridge north of Thrapston. The tower has often been described as one of the best in the country. There is both twelfth and thirteenth century fabric in the building. There is also a Norman zigzag arch in the chancel and the north arcade and north chapel are thirteenth century.

Several interesting features are worth mentioning. The room over the south porch was at one time connected to the manor by an overhead passage. The manor, demolished during the eighteenth century was then situated close to the church. There are paintings in the church by Mrs Creed, John Dryden's cousin. The poet often visited her spending much of his childhood in Titchmarsh. There are several monuments to the Pickering and Dryden families. The memorial on the wall in the north transept is to Erasmus Dryden and Mary Pickering and mentions at great length the poet.

The River Nene at **WADENHOE** broadens out and divides into two with one of its channels rushing over the ford beside the old mill. This ford gives access to the island by the river. The mill has been on the site since Saxon times and provides a picturesque setting for the village which climbs up the hill from the river The church of **ST MICHAEL** is in an isolated position outside the village and on a hill overlooking the river. The Norman tower had a saddleback roof added later. The circular font, the north arcade and chancel are all thirteenth century (Early English) and therefore added shortly after the Norman building.

SAINT ANDREWS CHURCH, BARNWELL is a beautiful traditional one with a strange south porch entrance, where the pillars supporting the archway actually lean outwards. Within the wide gable angle is an ancient sundial. The chancel in the main part of the church dates from the late thirteenth and early fourteenth centuries and is

all that remains of the original building. The combined restoration work of 1853 and 1873 has created today's church. Amidst the Decorated, Perpendicular and Jacobean styles of architecture there lies a monument high in the wall in the south-east corner of the chancel to Nicholas Latham, vicar of Barnwell from 1569 to 1620. As you can see from the almshouses opposite the church, he gave much to the village.

This is the church which Their Royal Highnesses the Duke and Duchess of Gloucester used to attend when they lived in Barnwell Manor. There is, on the south side of the chancel, a stone memorial in memory of 'His Royal Highness Prince Henry William Frederick Albert, Duke of Gloucester 1900-1974'. On the north aisle wall is a bronze memorial to Prince William of Gloucester, elder son of Their Royal Highnesses and brother of the present Duke. The memorial shows His Highness looking towards Barnwell Manor. Tragically he was killed taking part in an air race in 1973. There is also a wooden seat in the church porch which was given by his friends.

Before leaving the churchyard, follow the line of the church around towards the east and then to the north wall. Here, there is a fourteenth century door. At the base of the archstone and sitting on top of the shafted pillars you will find two rather strangely carved human heads. The westerly one (right-hand side), appears out of carved leaves and shows Jack O' the Green, a common effigy with masons of this period and derived from the old May Day customs and traditions.

Barnwell village originally grew out of two villages, each having its own church. Today the medieval church of **ALL SAINTS**, which was demolished in 1825, apart from the thirteenth century chancel, which stands isolated and forlorn, surrounded by its old graveyard. This is situated on the western side of the brook and is an interesting building full of montagu memorials.

THRAPSTON CHURCH OF ST JAMES, right, was probably built during the thirteenth century and it has strong Washington connections linking it with Sulgrave, Ecton and Islip. Sir John Washington, who was the second son of Lawrence Washington of Sulgrave, married a Mary Curtis of Islip. Sir John was Lord of the Manor of Thrapston and great, great, great uncle of the President of the United States. Inside the west

entrance to St James' Church and on the left is his coat of arms. Although dating from the thirteenth century only the chancel remains from this period.

ISLIP CHURCH OF ST NICHOLAS was built during the Perpendicular period of architecture and has a spire with lucarnes. The base of the tower is possibly twelfth century and therefore all that remains from an earlier church. The nave roof is supported by angels. The village stands on the west bank of the River Nene and close to the twelfth century bridge spanning the river. The church is important for its link with the American President for it is here that Sir John Washington's wife, Mary, is buried. There is a monument to her on the south wall of the sanctuary.

The **ADDINGTONS** lying south of Thrapston and just off the A605 consist of two villages, both with their own church.

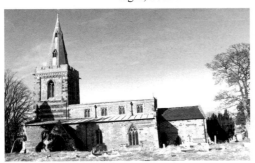

ST MARY'S, LITTLE ADDINGTON, left, was built during the thirteenth and fourteenth centuries with its short spire rising out of a massive tower. The west doorway of the tower is beautiful with its carvings and mouldings around the arches - look especially for the weather beaten figures on the inner arch. Look also at the chancel arch resting on the carved heads.

ALL SAINTS, GREAT ADDINGTON, below, was also built during the thirteenth and fourteenth centuries being initially dedicated in 1234, and the tower added in 1350. There was a Norman church on the site but only the south porchway remains with its characteristic zigzag mouldings. The manor was owned during the twelfth to sixteenth centuries by the de Vere family and there is a lovely plain tomb-chest with an alabaster figure to Henry de Vere who died in 1516 and who was the last in the family line.

ST MARY'S, WOODFORD stands proudly by the River Nene and was originally built during the Norman period and added to and remodelled shortly afterwards during the Early English period of architecture. The wall of the old Norman chancel was used in the nave and the south arcade was developed along the Norman style with large round arches and foliage on the capitals. A new north aisle, chancel and south porch with a room over it were added during the late thirteenth century. Other additions were made over the next two centuries including the octagonal spire. Explore

the church and find in the north aisle above the altar a memorial to Lady de Capell Brooke, two fourteenth century effigies in oak of a knight and lady and the strangest relic of all - a human heart! Inserted in one of the pillars on the north side of the nave is a glass case containing the remains of a human heart. This was found during church restoration in the 1860's and may be the heart of a knight killed at the crusades, but why would it be brought back to Woodford? Perhaps it was one of the Trailly family, killed at the crusades and who were Lords of the Manor 700 years ago? A mystery, probably never to be solved.

DENFORD situated adjacent to the river Nene and on the A605 south of Thrapston is an early church built mainly during the thirteenth century. The broached spire is recessed behind a parapet with pinnacles. The church has been restored but generally within the style of the original building. Above the sedilia in the chancel is a mysteri-

ous relieving arch with small holes in the tympanum, apparently made for acoustic jars to help with the resonance of the priests' voices.

RINGSTEAD village straddles the A605 just north of Raunds and along the valley of the Nene. **ST MARY'S CHURCH** was built during the thirteenth and fourteenth centuries and has a tower and broach spire from the earlier period with three tiers of lucarnes. Like many churches it was restored in the nineteenth century. There is a lovely example of a Decorated east window and look for the comic heads in the south porch and the carved heads looking down from the fourteenth century chancel.

Below: Doorways and arches, Woodnewton

ST MARY'S, WOODNEWTON has stood here since Norman times with the low tower re-built during the sixteenth century, although the Norman's, in planning a cruciform church were probably going to build the tower centrally. The priest's door is also of the earlier period. Look for further Norman architecture - the doorway into the south aisle and the arch leading into the south chapel.

The church dedicated to **ST MARY, SOUTHWICK** was built in the fourteenth century by John Knyvet, Chancellor of England, whilst he was living in the hall. It was later rebuilt and altered during the eighteenth and nineteenth centuries. The tower and nave arch remain from the original building. Look up inside the tower to see carved stones showing a king, queen and jester with the arms of the Knyvets on the tower.

Look on the floor of the chancel and see the magnificent black marble slab memorials to the Lynn family who also lived in the hall.

Outside the heavy buttress on the tower was needed as the ground on which the church now stands was the site of a Roman quarry and it was owing to the subsidence that the tower had to have the buttress added

ST LEONARD'S CHURCH, GLAPTHORN is very interesting mainly because of the thirteenth century architecture with a tower of the same period. The two western

bays of the south arcade are late Norman and the chancel is Early English but with an east window of 1300. The eastern bays of both nave arcades are Early English. There are three plain sixteenth century bench ends in the nave, and some fifteenth century panels and tracery are used in the chancel as reading-desks. There are interesting traces of wall paintings including one of St Christopher on the north wall of the north aisle. The font is of the late fourteenth or early fifteenth century. Look around for the piscina with dog tooth moulding. The south door and porch are of the fourteenth century. Also look for the Victorian bier for conveying the dead to the church.

A village of two parts **UPPER AND LOWER BENEFIELD** both sit on the main A427 Oundle to Corby road. The village takes its name from the lawns or open spaces

in the forest of Rockingham. During Henry III's reign a castle was built to the west of the church by Nicholas of Bassingbourne in 1208, but by 1315 or even earlier was derelict. Traces of the moat and foundations were still discernible in 1913.

The church of **ST MARY**, which stands in **LOWER BENE-FIELD** and is entered through a beautiful lych gate, has been largely rebuilt during the nineteenth century except for the chancel which is probably fourteenth century. It's restoration is elaborate, with a modern well-carved rood-screen and figures. Here are some of the misericord stalls from Fotheringhay.
Look for a lion, a green man and a sprig of foliage.
There is a brass memorial to Elizabeth Grant, 1608. The reredos is from 1897. The sedilia and piscina have been restored but still retain their fourteenth century style. The poppyhead stalls fit in well with the medieval stalls. The font is of Caen stone whilst the floor of the whole church is laid in encaustic tiles; and are described by one writer as 'a perfect gem'. In 1904 a loft was added to the rood screen and a staircase added in 1906.

ST PETER'S CHURCH, LOWICK dominates the area, situated as it is on high ground with the tower and exquisitely carved stone lantern, drawing the eye upwards. The church was largely built by the Greene family during the Perpendicular period but in particular during the late fourteenth and early fifteenth centuries. You must explore the church and discover the variety of tombs and memorials to the Green family - perhaps start with the tomb of

Ralph Greene and his wife. They are in the arch between the chancel and the north chapel and then see the brass portrait of Henry Greene in the south chapel and depicted in full armour. Other tombs remember the Earl of Wiltshire (1499) and the Earl of Dorset, both fascinating to see and admire - the former in the south chapel is considered one of the best pieces of fifteenth century carving to be found. Spend time exploring the church - there is much to see and admire.

BRIGSTOCK parish church of **ST ANDREW** is undoubtedly one of the most magnificent with rich Saxon remains including the rare example of a stair-turret. This, the base of the great tower, and the great arch leading through from the nave to the tower, all remain intact and date back to AD850-900. Although the church was destroyed by the Danes, it was soon rebuilt and during the Norman times the north aisle was added, followed by the south aisle in the twelfth century. Throughout the following centuries the church was widened and extended, the south porch added, windows and arches designed and built, all in the style of the period. In 1873 the church was completely restored, Although the medieval roof has not survived there is a medieval screen (supposedly from Pipewell Abbey), separating the Lady Chapel from the north aisle. In this chapel there is a mutilated niche which once contained a statue of the Virgin Mary. This was smashed by Cromwell's soldiers, presumably during the Civil War. Look for the marble tomb of Robert Vernon, Lord Lyveden and in the government at the time of the Crimean War.

As you leave the church by the south door, notice the monk's door on the right. This door led to a room over the porch which was the living quarters of the priest monk from Cirencester. Finally, look for the sundial over the porch and walk along the path and bridge over the river (Harpers Brook) for a better view of the church and turret.

John Dryden who became the Poet Laureate in 1670 was born in **ALDWINKLE** in 1631 and there is a memorial in the church to the poet. Aldwinkle is an unusual village in that for many years it had two churches, **ST PETERS and ALL SAINTS.**

ALL SAINTS, where the Dryden memorials are, is now closed and part of the Redundant Churches Scheme but the interior is mainly thirteenth century and the exterior fifteenth century. Look for the carved heads and figures in the tower.

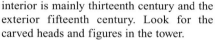

ST PETER'S, left, church has architecture dating from several periods beginning with the west pier of the north arcade which is late twelfth century. There is considerable thirteenth century fabric and the south window has remains of fourteenth century glass, especially St Christopher and St George. The broach spire is reputed to be one of the best in the county.

Wellingborough & Surrounding Villages

Wellingborough stands at the junction of two rivers, the Nene and Ise. During the tenth century the invading Saxons moved along the Nene settling on defensive hilltops and in fertile areas close to the river. On one such ridge is Earls Barton and All Saints church is regarded as having the finest Saxon tower in England, dated around 970 AD.

As the shoe industry gathered momentum during the second half of the nineteenth century local towns expanded including, Wellingborough, Earls Barton, Irthlingborough, Raunds, Finedon, Wollaston and Higham Ferrers. This expansion continued through to Kettering, Rothwell and Dseborough following the opening of the railway in 1857. The local village churches, all worth visiting, emerge with interesting local and national stories to recount.

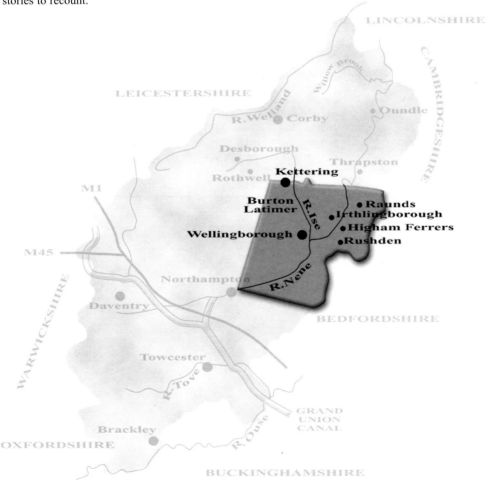

J. COX.

he **PARISH CHURCH OF ALL HALLOWS, WELLINGBOROUGH**. has a thirteenth century spire, rising to a height of 165 feet which dominates the surrounding area. Like so many of Northampton's churches, All Hallows was originally Saxon, but probably suffered at the hands of the marauding Danes. The south doorway is Norman with almost all the rest of the church being built during the thirteenth and fourteenth centuries. Small additions were then made in the following centuries. In the chancel is a set of beautifully carved misericords, and the stained glass windows are worth looking at, especially the two west windows, one of these being designed by John Piper. A sad tale is told in a window in the north aisle of a Thomas Jones, rector of the church, who was a staunch Royalist and during the Civil War was twice thrown in prison for his beliefs. On one occasion he was put on the back of a bear and dragged by soldiers to Northampton. Eventually he died in prison.

WILBY village straddles the A4500 about a mile from Wellingborough and on the Northampton road. The church of **ST MARY** has quite an unusual and unique tower. Built during the Decorated period it has a square base with diagonal buttresses developing into an octagonal shape with pinnacles. Further pinnacles and buttresses lead to the spire. The nave retains a thirteenth century south arcade and the east window is from the same period, with clerestory windows about a hundred years later. The chancel was rebuilt in 1753, and a north vestry added in 1873 and the church was restored in 1879. As you leave look for the four gargoyles on the tower.

WOLLASTON church is dedicated to the **BLESSED VIRGIN MARY** and is one of the county's cruciform churches where the tower and Decorated spire are in the centre of the church with the aisles, transepts, nave and chancel having all been built out from the centre of the cross. Most of the church fell down in November 1735 and was rebuilt over the next two years and only the tower and north transept remain from the original structure. The central tower and spire are very fine examples of work of the Decorated period. The tower rests on four tall pointed arches between the chancel and the nave. Look around the base of the piers of brown stone and see the numbers one, three, five and seven. These are reputed to have been put there by the builders in 1357 and the numbers therefore represent the date the church was built. The pulpit is dated 1737 and was part of an old three tiered pulpit. The font dates from the same time.

ST KATHERINE'S CHURCH, IRCHESTER, left, was built of ironstone and limestone during the thirteenth and fourteenth centuries and the spire with three tiers of lucarnes (windows) dominates the village. Although restored over the years much of the original building remains and there are traces of a medieval doom painting over the chancel arch. Explore the church and look at the thirteenth century font with its carvings. Also find the church oven in the north wall of the chancel. Bread would have been baked here for use at communion. Look and admire the stained glass windows but two in particular. The east window of the south aisle shows the Baptism in the River Jordan of John the Baptist and the east window of the north aisle shows the life of St Katherine, the latter is quite a moving story and the window is a blaze of colour. Katherine stands crowned in the centre with a palm in one hand and the other resting on a wheel and around her are four main panels depicting her life including kneeling before her execution and the angels accepting her into Heaven. As you leave the church notice the weathervane which incorporates a catherine wheel, which is supposed to have been the instrument of torture on which Saint Katherine met her death.

ST JOHN THE BAPTIST, STRIXTON was originally a thirteenth century church but was completely rebuilt along the lines of the previous church during the late nineteenth century and it is said that the stone from the old church was used to rebuild the new one, although this has never been proven. The church has a bellcote at the west end with a saddleback roof. Although there are other churches with a saddleback roof we think that this church is unique in the county as having both a bellcote tower and saddleback roof combined. During the rebuilding the tomb of a priest in the south wall was found and contained a skeleton and altar vessels, the latter probably being his own. In the thickness of the west wall we find a staircase leading to the belfry. Most of the windows are paired lancets and the west doorway has a fourteenth century arch with a rare circular window above it.

HIGHAM FERRERS, a small town, standing on the A6 just outside Rushden. The busy main road hides a wealth of medieval heritage and memorials to a famous son - Henry Chichele, who became Archbishop of Canterbury. From the central market place go through the passage leading into the medieval setting around the church. So peaceful and tranquil is the setting that it is reminiscent of a cathedral city.

The church was already here when Henry Chichele was born in the parish in 1362, but the Bede House and Chantry School were inspired and built by him. The church of the **BLESSED VIRGIN MARY** was constructed in the thirteenth and fourteenth centuries. Much was destroyed during the sixteenth century resulting in extensive restoration during the 1860s. There is plenty to see and admire, starting with the west entrance and porch. Outside, above the door, are ten circular 'medallion type' carvings richly depicting in great detail the life of Christ. For instance, *The Visitation, The Wise Men and Christ at Calvary.*

The tower with its spire was initially built between 1250 and 1280 and added to in 1631. It rises 170 feet and is a magnificent spectacle, dominating the town and surrounding buildings. The church is a large spacious building with many treasures. The octagonal font is of the thirteenth century. Hanging on the north wall beside it is a suit of pike armour of the sixteenth century. This, together with other armour, was probably bought by the borough to fulfil a government demand to defend the town should this be necessary.

Moving through to the east end of the church, you will see the Lady Chapel adjacent to the chancel. In both these sections of the church there are brass floor-memorials to several of the Chichele family, but not to William. There is a tomb chest which divides the Lady Chapel from the chancel, and which is thought by many to be one of the finest brasses to a parish priest in the country. It is a memorial to Laurence de Saneto Mauro (Seymour), who was rector of Higham Ferrers from 1298 to 1337. Read the additional notes by the tomb and look at the canopy and see the beautiful carvings.

The frontal on the High Altar provides a symbolic link with the local shoe and leather trade. The leather was tanned locally and then made into an altar frontal and presented by John White, a local shoe factory, and blessed by the Bishop of Peterborough in 1970. The chancel also has misericord choir seats carved with lions, pelicans, angels and others.

Henry Chichele was a scholar at Winchester and Oxford. He was ordained priest in 1396 and was Archbishop of Canterbury from 1414 until he died in 1443. He became very rich and was responsible for the building of the Chantry School and the Bede House.

The **CHAPEL CHANTRY,** built around 1460, is situated outside the west door and was used as a grammar school until 1912. Although not built in his life time, Chichele commissioned the Perpendicular style building. The chapel looks like a miniature version of Kings College Chapel, Cambridge, and it is said that Lord Vaux of Harrowden admired it so much that he built an identical one for himself. Today this is in the grounds of Wellingborough Golf Club and can be seen quite clearly from the road.

In 1428 Chichele founded the **BEDEHOUSE,** or Hospital, as a home for twelve elderly men. It is built in attractive, striped and alternating courses of ironstone and limestone. Chichele provided each old man with a one penny a day pension, free fuel and special clothing. 'Bede' means 'prayer' and it was the duty of these men to pray for their king and the founders of the charity and to abide by a strict set of rules. The eastern end of the house was raised and used as a chapel. The main door of the Bedehouse is open enabling you to see the building from inside the porch.

Accompanying these fine buildings in the churchyard is the fourteenth century cross and more recently a war memorial which has been fixed to the top, a Crucifix on one side and a figure of the Virgin Mary on the other. Finally if you wish to visit the possible site of Chichele's birthplace walk along the south side of the High Street towards Rushden and a plaque on the wall marks the cottage.

RUSHDEN, now a small town has developed through the shoe industry and has a church dedicated to **ST MARY** sitting centrally on a large island on the A6. The beautiful 164 foot crocketed spire has pierced flying buttresses and pinnacles and three tiers of lucarnes, all allowing light to permeate through. A glorious sight, and inside the church shows off its glory. There is a fifteenth century roof supported by angels and some of the stained glass is also fifteenth century, together with the screens. The pulpit is medieval and has the dreaded hour glass!! The bowl of the font is thirteenth century and the stem of the next century. Explore the memorials, especially to the Pemberton family where we have two kneeling figures facing each other across a prayer desk, with the children kneeling at the base.

RAUNDS is a town that has grown out of the nineteenth century shoe industry and the church of **ST MARY** has many interesting features, including the tower and spire soaring 183 feet upwards - a true symbol of the phrase, 'Northamptonshire, a county of squires and spires'. The church has been in existence since the Normans, with evidence in a window above the south arcade and within the nave itself. The tower was added around 1225 and the south doorway and beautiful east window were also there in the thirteenth century. There is the possibility that the font with its ram's head sticking out was also of this period. The church continued to develop including the medieval wall paintings in the nave, chancel, in the north aisle and over the north doorway. Within these paintings look for St Christopher, St Catherine, angels and Pride and her six children. There are also memorial brasses, tombs and monuments.

IRTHLINGBOROUGH is now almost a town, but often described as an 'industrialised village', due to the development of the shoe industry and other light industrial factories. It is also the home of the Nene Park Complex and Rushden & Diamonds Football Club. Situated just off the new A45, a few miles from Wellingborough and alongside the River Nene the 'village' church of **ST PETER** has interesting beginnings. The local manor was bought by John Pyle in 1354 and in 1373 he became Mayor of London. In 1388 his widow founded a college in Irthlingborough, having obtained a licence in 1375 to make the building a church collegiate. The tower survives from this collegiate and was probably built perhaps as early as 1354 when John Pyle obtained the manor. The tower which was built of ironstone and grey stone had to be rebuilt towards the end of the nineteenth century after it began to lean. It is likely that prior to John Pyle building the tower that there was a thirteenth century church, probably in the form of a nave as there is evidence of an earlier building. For instance some of the chancel columns rest on Norman bases. The church continued to expand and there are Decorated windows with flowing tracery and much of the chancel is thirteenth century. There is much to explore and admire in the church. The stained glass windows, the eight surviving stalls with poppyheads, and the monuments and memorials. Admire the unique craftsmanship with the beautiful tomb of John and his wife, showing shields and angels together with two alabaster figures and the tomb to the left of the altar which is thought to be the first wife of Thomas Cheney who carried on the work of John Pyle.

ST PETER'S CHURCH, ISHAM stands majestically by the main Wellingborough to Kettering road and the church dates from the twelfth century. You can find work of almost every architectural period here including Norman and Early English. In the choir stalls look for two misericords and poppyhead pews and in the nave to find a Norman capital with four heads and foliage coming from their mouths. The fourteen candle holder chandelier near the altar dates from just after the battle of Waterloo and hangs above the seventeenth century altar rail. The pulpit is a fine example of carved oak from the Jacobean period and is guarded by angels with their wings outstretched. The square medieval tower has a frieze of panelling below the battlements with monsters looking out from each corner. An unusual aspect to the church is that the tower with its six bells, also has at the east end of the nave a sanctus bellcote tower, although it has no bell.

ST MARY'S CHURCH, ORLINGBURY was completely rebuilt in 1843 on the site of the old building which had fallen into decay and was too dangerous to use. The church dominates the village green and which is close to the Wellingborough to Kettering road. There is a rose window at the east end of the church. Many memorials and monuments from the old church have been transferred to the new. There is an alabaster effigy of a knight, 1375, who is said to be Jack Badsaddle and his claim to fame is that he is supposed to have killed the last wolf in England close to the church and was injured in the process. He crawled to a nearby stream, drank the cold waters and died - a tall story perhaps, who knows? Several monuments in the church are to the Young family who lived in the hall during the eighteenth century.

ST MARY'S CHURCH, LITTLE HARROWDEN has the larger building of the two Harrowdens and has a quite spectacular south Norman doorway showing the characteristic zig-zag mouldings. The Norman church was very basic and bays and aisles were added during the following two centuries with a medieval chancel screen. The church spire fell down in a violent storm in 1703 and the church was restored in 1851. The Norman tower became unsafe and had to be demolished in 1967, subsequently a vestry was built with an arch and one bell on the roof.

PYTCHLEY, close to Kettering has a church dating back to the Norman period with an Early English tower, to which the upper story was added in 1427. The church dedicated to **ALL SAINTS** has a remarkably broad north aisle. Indeed the church is rather large for a village, probably due to the numbers living here during the nineteenth century heyday of the hall,

St Mary's, Little Harrowden and Norman doorway.

mansions and building of the Midland Railway, when many of the work force lived in Pytchley. Much of the church was built during the thirteenth and fourteenth centuries and then restored and remodelled during the nineteenth century. The south arcade dates from 1230-40, but the eastern portion of the north arcade is some fifty years later and the old roof has grotesque corbels. The font basin is circular and is reputed to be Norman, it was dug up in the churchyard in 1838 and placed in the church on a modern pedestal. There is a Jacobean pulpit of oak. There is a solid panelled screen across the vestry arch and at the west end of the church we find an oak table dated 1704 and a dug out chest of oak in the south aisle.

HARDWICK village with its few houses lies just outside Wellingborough between the Kettering and Northampton roads. **ST LEONARD'S** built around 1200 is small and compact with a thirteenth century tower and battlements. A clerestory was added on the south side in the fourteenth century and in 1795 the chancel was shortened by eight feet, the aisle taken down, and a new south wall erected blocking the arcade, which was incorporated within the new wall and a south porch was also erected. In 1866 the arcade was opened out and the aisle rebuilt, a north porch added, the east wall of the chancel reconstructed, and the whole church re-roofed. At the restoration of the chancel the original east-end foundation was found, but the wall was rebuilt on its eighteenth century foundation. The font is thirteenth century and is one of the most interesting in the county. The bowl is set within six plain arches on rounded columns, reaching from the base almost to the top. Each arch having a plain background has a recess shaped like a window. There are brasses to the Nicolls and Bagshawe families. On the south wall there is a monument to Sir Francis Nicolls, who lived at the manor, his wife and their son and daughter all kneeling. Sir Francis was Governor of Tilbury Fort at the time of the Armada and died in 1621. The pulpit dates from around 1860 and is made of Derbyshire Spa inlaid with mosaic and has a design of the Good Shepherd.

The church of **ALL SAINTS, GREAT HARROWDEN** sits on the main Kettering road just outside Wellingborough and close to Wellingborough Golf Club which is situated in the late Harrowden Hall, the home of the Vaux family for over 400 years. The church has traces of a twelfth century foundation with the remains of a Norman window in the west wall of the nave, although it may even be older. The current fabric is largely of the Decorated period and the tower, the spire which had been added later, collapsed in the eighteenth century and was rebuilt in 1822. The chancel was rebuilt a few years later but look above the screen to find a faded medieval wall painting. Look in the chancel for the brass memorial to William of Harrowden who died in 1434 and to his wife Margaret, their son married into the Vaux family who built Harrowden Hall - now the golf club. Outside around the outer walls you will find a selection of interesting gargoyles.

FINEDON, a village on the outskirts of Wellingborough with a large church dedicated to **ST MARY** and built during the Decorated period (1280-1350). Built out of iron-

J. R. COX 1985

stone with grey stone dressings the church is particularly beautiful with a lovely east window, a great arch across the nave, stone faces and gargoyles around the church, and a south porch with a vaulted roof and a room above supported by four gargoyles The font is Norman and has a carved battered Annunciation. Look at the memorials and in particular the one below the east window which is the Dolben family vault.

EARLS BARTON CHURCH is situated on the top of a hill overlooking the village and offered an accessible refuge in times of trouble. It has, perhaps, the finest Saxon tower in Britain.

Built in AD970, probably on the site of an earlier wooden church, the distinctive Saxon tower has no buttresses or stairway but pilaster strips which are a feature of late Anglo-Saxon architecture. These narrow bands of stonework project a few centimetres beyond the surfaces, giving the appearance of half-timbered framework.

Having admired the tower, which is over a thousand years old, step inside the church and find the evidence of Norman architecture. In 1086 the Domesday Book recalls the village of Buartone as having a church dedicated to **ALL SAINTS**. In the twelfth century the Earl of Northampton, Simon de Senlis, built the Norman nave. Find the beautiful Norman arcading either side of the chancel and, when you return outside, look

closely at the Norman doorway and their carvings. Earls Barton Church is fortunate to have been built by successive generations and there are examples of church architecture for every period. The highly decorated medieval fifteenth century rood screen, having been restored in the nineteenth century, is a splendid colourful spectacle. It was repainted during the nineteenth century and depicts the saints in 'modern' costume, above which are an array of brilliant butterflies. In the middle ages the rood cross was the most important part of the church. Candles were erected on the candle beam in front of the rood cross to draw people's eyes up to the cross upon entering the church.

Before returning outside through the Norman doorway look for other typical

J. COX 88

period features - the sixteenth century Jacobean carved oak pulpit, the fourteenth century aisle windows of the decorated period. Can you find the scratch dials on the south aisle wall outside? These old-style, roughly-carved sundials are often found on the south walls of churches or on churchyard crosses.

The village of **GREAT DODDINGTON** lying on the old Wellingborough road is thought to date back to the Iron Age with traces of hut circles, storage pits and ditches. **ST NICHOLAS' CHURCH** is old with the lower part of the tower being Norman and the top eighteenth century. The double shafted west doorway is very Early English and the rest of the church is fourteenth century, including the chancel sedilia. Explore the misericord carvings, one of which shows artists at work and the Jacobean pulpit with a wrought iron hour glass (1618) - the 'sermon timer'!

ECTON Village is a pilgrimage for all Americans as Benjamin Franklin's ancestors  lived here for over three hundred years. For generations the Franklins were the village blacksmiths and their smithy was in the High Street where the Three Horseshoes Inn now stands. The smithy was burned down, but parts of the old structure are to be found in the yard behind the inn. The last in line in Ecton was Thomas who died on 6 January 1702. He is buried with his wife Eleanor a few yards from the north porch and also nearby is a tree planted as a memorial to Benjamin. Thomas and his wife were uncle and aunt to Benjamin, so it was with interest that Benjamin visited the village in 1758. His father was born in Ecton but emigrated to Boston, Massachusetts in 1682. In the church there is a bronze plaque on the wall in the north aisle and near to the vestry.

Before leaving the church of **ST MARY MAGDALENE** spend a while looking around. The first stone church was built here over eight hundred years ago, although there was one before that of Saxon origin. An unusual inscription giving the date when the old part of the church was built can be found on a left hand pillar outside the north porch. This type of inscription is unusual:

A m cccclvj edificatur
"built in the year of Our Lord 1456"

Also in the north porch above the doorway is a beautifully carved Calvary group which includes the figure of Mary Magdalene, to whom the church is dedicated. Inside the church are several huge memorial tablets on the north and south sides of the church walls. If you look closely you will also see where the rood loft separating the chancel from the nave would have been. The font at the back of the church is probably fourteenth century and having been lost for about three hundred years was found in a local farmyard being used as a trough!

Finally, as you walk back through the churchyard, look back at the thirteenth century tower to see how the lower part was built of sandstone and then, a century later, a pale limestone top was added.

ST PETER AND ST PAUL, SYWELL was probably built between the twelfth and fourteenth centuries using Northamptonshire ironstone, but restored, including the rebuilding of the chancel around 1862 to 1870. Retained in the chancel is the medieval piscina. The late thirteenth century tower with an interesting stair projection on the west wall, rests on its original Norman foundations and a Norman tower arch and Norman arcade with three huge pillars. Look for the grim looking gargoyles around the

tower. The original south doorway was probably late twelfth century and the recessed tomb in the north transept was fourteenth century. The east window is really worth a study with its beautiful Elizabethan glass and tiny coloured figures. There are many monuments to the Pell family who succeeded the Wilmers at Sywell Hall. One of the most beautiful features of the church is the peace memorial window designed by Christopher Whall. It has four lights and shows Joshua outside the walls of Jericho, note the lovely scenery in the background of the window depicting sun, moon and stars. An unusual feature of the church are its two fonts, but the thirteenth century one found in the local field is still used. Sywell is an old, modernised church situated in the old village, surrounded by cottages, many of which were built by Lord and Lady Overstone during the Victorian era, when they had amassed one of the biggest fortunes in England. On the green outside the church the old preaching cross now forms part of the Jubilee Memorial of the Victorian era.

OVERSTONE, about four miles from Northampton and just off the A43 Kettering road is a long linear village with the church of **ST NICHOLAS**, built in 1807 and remodelled in 1903, standing in a field in Overstone Park a short walk from the village. The church built by John Kipling replaced the old dilapidated earlier one built in 1222. There are no traces of this first church which stood in front of the manor house and during the fifteenth century had four altars dedicated to the Saints, Mary, Anne, Thomas and John the Baptist. The north wall of St Nicholas' holds the 'Wantage Window', below. Lady Wantage once owned the manor and gave the window in memory of her husband who fought in the Crimean War, winning one of the first VC crosses to be awarded. There are also several wall plaques from the old church.

The church of **ALL SAINTS, MEARS ASHBY** is situated in the centre of the village just off the A4500 Northampton to Wellingborough road and has many interesting features to look for and explore. The church was probably here around 1100 and the magnificent Norman font greets you as you enter through the Norman south doorway. Whilst the church has been restored over the years, two other features must be seen. In the south aisle is an old Saxon 'Wheel Cross', according to historians, possibly of Viking origin, dated around AD1000 and may have been the mark of a pre-conquest burial place. These crosses are normally found in the north of England and are a rarity so far south. The other feature not to be missed is the 'Doom Painting' above the chancel arch and restored in 1984.

ST MARY'S, GREAT HOUGHTON, next page - top left, was built in 1754 replacing an earlier one built during the thirteenth century.
ST MARY'S, LITTLE HOUGHTON, next page - top right, was first built by William de Houghton in 1100. William was Chamberlain to Henry I and also Lord of

the Manor. There are no visible remains of this first church and a new one was built during the thirteenth and fourteenth centuries. The tower was completed during this period and the south porch has a Norman doorway. The circular font is also, either Norman or a good imitation! Look for the medieval piscina and misericord with carvings of men's heads and monsters as arm pieces. The church was re-built in the 1870's but retained many of its key features including the tower and the tower and chancel arch.

ST LAWRENCE CHURCH, BRAFIELD dates back to the Norman period with the lower part of the tower probably from this period and then added to about a hundred and fifty years later during the Perpendicular period. Look around the tower for gargoyles and rows of iron studs. The chancel was rebuilt in 1848 and not much of the original remains, although the south arcade with some carvings is possibly Early English. Finally before leaving admire the large Norman font.

ST PETER'S CHURCH, COGENHOE has an interesting early history. The church was built during the thirteenth and fourteenth centuries initially by Nicholas de Cogenhoe who completed it in 1280. Further additions followed by William de Cogenhoe. The Cogenhoe's owned the local estate and the heir died at the young age of !0 years. Agnes, his sister, and last of the Cogenhoe line built the tower as a memorial to her young brother in 1380. During the nineteenth century the church was restored but it retained many of its earlier features. Look at the north and south doorways, the thirteenth century chancel, animal heads supporting the roof, the tower and the windows. Find Nicholas de Cogenhoe's effigy it is thought that he was a Crusader as the effigy shows him as a knight with his characteristic crossed legs.

ST MARY'S, WHISTON, lying between Cogenhoe and Castle Ashby is situated on a hill behind the village. It appears that the church was probably built by Anthony Catesby over a fairly short time, possibly thirty years and probably around the 1530's. The solid tower built of ironstone and limestone is elaborately decorated with carved figures and pinnacles. Look for the demons, angels, monkeys and gargoyles on the tower. Further angel corbels are found inside. There are several interesting monuments including one to Thomas Catesby and to the First (1775) and Second Lord Boston (1835). Several of these are standing scenic monuments.

ST MARGARET'S, DENTON lies in the centre of the village and has a thirteenth century tower and chancel, both being retained during the early nineteenth century rebuilding. Inside the church is wider than it is long and there is a west gallery. A strange coal store on the south side, also has a blocked opening into the church and it has been suggested that it might have been an anchoress's cell.

ST MARY MAGDALENE, CASTLE ASHBY lies adjacent to Castle Ashby House and the home of the Earl of Northampton. The church was restored in the 1800's but still shows a late Norman or Early English north doorway with the characteristic zigzag arch and dogtooth mouldings. Much of the rest of the church is of the Decorated and Perpendicular period of architecture. The tower, chancel and south aisle are Perpendicular with the north aisle of the Decorated period.

The church, although overshadowed by the house has a superb brass of the fourteenth century rector William Ermy, many Compton monuments and then later monuments to the Marquess and Marchioness of Northampton - the first in 1828. The Castle was in ruins when Sir William Compton bought the estate in 1512. The building of the house began in 1574. Also look around the churchyard for the monuments and in particular four life sized praying angels.

ST ANDREW'S, YARDLEY HASTINGS has a massive short thirteenth century tower, but the church began life during the Norman period. Some historians suggest that the tower is Norman with the arches in the chancel wall having been blocked in by the Early English builders. The nave is wide and has four arches on each side and possibly the south door is Early English together with the chancel arches. The beautiful east window in the chancel is medieval and the modern glass depicts the four stages of Our Lord's Life - Birth, Death, Resurrection and Ascension. Perhaps there should have been five - Our Lord's Life. Look for the carvings around the chancel - the head of a queen, a scowling face and figure with fingers stretching open a mouth - medieval toothache?! There are several interesting monuments around the church, including the local schoolmaster and rectors.

STANWICK CHURCH, below, dedicated to **ST LAWRENCE** stands majestic on the sweep of the road with the lovely tall pine trying to out grow the magnificent octagonal tower. The church was built during the Early English period and the spire emerging naturally out of the tower reaches a height of 153 feet and some years ago was described, 'as a valuable gem of Northamptonshire church architecture'. One of the

bells still ringing in the tower is dated 1360 and the font is also from this period with the richly carved bowl and pedestal and a strange carved foot. Spend time to look at the windows and the memorials and the pulpit, the latter given to the church in the sixteenth century by John Dolben whose father was rector here. John, born at the rectory later became Archbishop of York. Finally as you leave note the upper room in the porch, possibly where the priest used to live.

GRENDON CHURCH, next page - top right, dedicated to **ST MARY** stands proudly in the village overlooking the Nene valley with its Perpendicular tower and battlemented nave. Gargoyles are around the tower and two horrible looking corbels are on the chancel arch. They are supposed to be husband and wife glaring horribly at each other! A family feud! The two western bays of the arcades and the south doorway are Norman and there is some Early English work in each aisle. The rest of the nave is from the Decorated period.

On the left as you enter the church is the square Victorian lead lined font with four columns and the first four columns in the aisle with the decorated capitals represent the first smaller church of the twelfth century. The hatchments on the wall are of the Compton family who used to live at Grendon Hall. They were displayed outside the house of the deceased and then brought into the church for safe keeping. Note the right hand one has ravens on it representing the arms of the Lord Lieutenant of the Tower of London.

ST PETER AND ST PAUL, EASTERN MAUDIT consists of a nave and side aisles with a chancel and south porch. The tower with flying buttresses and a beautiful spire was added later. The church was built in its present form in the fourteenth century and then altered in 1832, with further restoration in 1859-61. The fourteenth century south doorway retains its ancient oak door and the magnificent eighteenth century font rests on a square base. There is a medieval piscina and an elaborately carved seventeenth altar table.

The church is known for its illustrious associations with the world of theatre, literature and national statesmen. Thomas Percy became vicar during the eighteenth century at the age of twenty four and who later became a national figure in the world of poetry producing several published anthologies. Percy was vicar here between 1753 and 1782 and later became a bishop. David Garrick 1717-79, an English actor worshipped here as did more recently David Nimmo. Look around the pews to find a brass plaque which reads:

> *Ss Peter and Paul*
> *Dr S Johnson*
> *O Goldsmith*
> *D Garrick*
> *Worshipped here in*
> *this pew with other*
> *members of the*
> *Garrick Club*

In the north chapel there are beautiful monuments to the Yelverton family whose mansion was destroyed in the early nineteenth century. Sir Christopher Yelvertoft, Judge, actor and Speaker of the House of Commons died in 1612 and is still remembered because he composed and read daily the beautiful prayer which is still used at every sitting of the House of Commons. At his side is the more imposing memorial of his son, Sir Henry who died 1631 and his wife, supported by two bedesman in black gowns and white beards.

BOZEAT situated on the A509 Wellingborough to Olney road and the church of **ST MARY** was first built during the Norman period dating around 1130, although there was probably an earlier church on the site. The Norman tower was rebuilt around the 1880's using much of the same material and the doorway, chancel lancet and priest's door were built during the thirteenth century. In the chancel, (restored both in 1874 and 1895), we find a beautifully decorated chancel screen with paintings over 500 years old. Paintings include the Expulsion of Adam and Eve from the Garden of Eden, the Annunciation, the Adoration of the Magi and the Baptism. In the fifteenth century they added the clerestory

windows and the solid main beams of the roof and it is said that the pews were built of the same timbers on which the parishioners have sat for over 550 years. At the east end of the north arcade the circular staircase to the rood loft remains with its lower and upper doorways. You will find brackets, canopies and piscinas at the end of each aisle, showing the former existence of altars.

The largely thirteenth century church of **ST JOHN THE BAPTIST** serves both the communities of **CALDECOTE AND CHELVESTON**. The original structure of nave and aisles is Early English and even the clerestory retains simple lancets, which is most unusual. The south aisle has three light Decorated windows. Look between the south aisle and the Chapel to find an arch resting on a beautifully carved fourteenth century head with its mouth stretched out, and with leaves above the head. You will see that the tower is in the north side of the church - most unusual as most towers or steeples are on the west end and opposite the high altar. It may be that the ground was too soft to support a tower in its usual place and this is mostly substantiated by the thickness of the walls, in some places five feet thick. Due to the dilapidated state of the fabric the church had to be closed and was restored during the nineteenth century. The church also had a new north aisle added and was reopened in 1849 - interestingly the cost at the time was £726 of which the parishioners had to provide £410. Look for the plaque dedicated to the men from the nearby airbase who lost their lives during the Second World War.

Blocked up priest's doorway, Hargrave.

HARGRAVE. A fascinating and interesting church dedicated to **ALL SAINTS** with a thirteenth century tower, nineteenth century 90 foot broach spire and a circular stair turret. The present church dates from the twelfth century although it is thought that an earlier wooden one was in existence. Look and admire the medieval fresco of St Christopher on the north wall of the nave and the poor box carved out of oak by a villager in 1597. It is also suggested that the base of the font was once used as a Roman Altar. Also look for the stone on which are scratched the lines used in playing the game of Nine Men's Morris, it is thought that this was perhaps built into the wall as long ago as the twelfth century. Today the game can be found in certain toy shops. Also look outside for the unusually large stone coffin approximately 7 feet long and 2 feet wide. It was found, with a skeleton in and other Roman remains in a field nearby.

A macabre story is recounted of a local farmer by the name of Dunham, who lived at Three-Shire House, and who kept the body of his wife and his daughter for some years in a small adjoining house as he was not allowed to inter his wife's remains within the church!

NEWTON BROMSWOLD village with its spire of **ST PETER** rising above the farmland is mainly of the Decorated and Perpendicular period and is quite remarkable for such a small church, in that we find six sedilia (priest's seats) in the chancel. Below the parapet on the south wall is a series of flowers, faces and shields and you will find a head on each corner. Look around the glass and see the mitred figure possibly of Archbishop Chichele, who was born locally in Higham Ferrers in 1362 or, as others speculate Hugh of Lincoln - whichever is correct the window is a fine example of medieval stained glass with a rare blue flowered pattern background. There are brasses to former rectors William Hewet of 1426 and Robert Hewet of 1487. The chancel screen is in memory of those who fell in the First World War and the fourteenth century font is an octagonal bowl and has carvings on six sides. Look in the churchyard and to the south-east of the porch where there is a remnant of the base of an old churchyard cross.

APPENDIX 1

GLOSSARY

ABACUS	a slab at the top of a capital.
AISLE	wing or passage; the sideways extension of the church.
APSE	vaulted semicircle end of the chapel or chancel.
ARCADE	series of arches supported by columns.
ASHLAR	masonry or stones in regular courses.
BATTLEMENT	parapet with a series of indentations, often like a castle wall.
BELFRY	turret on a roof to hang bells in.
BELLCOTE	a small tower built on the roof usually holding one bell.
BOX PEW	a pew enclosed by high wooden back and ends with a door, farmers and Lord's of the Manor often had their own box pew.
BUTTRESS	masonry built against a wall to strengthen it or resist the ou ward thrust of an arch.
CAPITAL	the top part of a column.
CASTELLATED	decorated battlements.
CHANCEL	the place where the altar is situated, usually the east end of the church.
CHANCEL ARCH	the arch at the west end of the chancel, normally walked through to reach the chancel.
CHANTRY	place used for prayer or saying mass.
CHOIR	part of the church where the service is sung.
CLERESTORY	upper part of a nave wall with windows usually above the aisle.
CORBEL	block of stone projecting from a wall, often with features of a face or animal
CROCKETING	decorative features placed on sloping sides of spires.
CRYPT	underground room usually beneath the east end of a church.
DOGTOOTH	typical Early English ornament consisting of a series of four -cornered stars.
EASTER SEPULCHRE	recess with tomb-chest used for Easter celebrations.
FLYING BUTTRESS	an external arch springing over the roof of an aisle and supporting the wall of the clerestory.
FONT	usually at the west end of the church for baptisms, they were sometimes locked to prevent the holy water being stolen.
FRIEZE	decoration around a wall.
GARDEROBE	toilet in a medieval building.
GARGOYLE	waterspout projecting from a parapet or wall carved into a human or animal shape.
HAGIOSCOPE	a hole cut through a pier or wall to allow a view of the altar.
LUCARNE	a small opening to let light in, usually a window in a roof or spire.
LYCH GATE	a roofed gateway at the entrance to the graveyard, usually a place to rest the coffin, lych is Saxon and means corpse.
MISERICORD	a tip up seat in the choir stalls, frequently carved, on which the user might recline yet remain on his feet.
NAVE	the main body of the church.
NICHE	a vertical recess in a wall, sometimes for a statue.
ORATORY	a small private chapel.
PIER	a strong solid support.
PINNACLE	ornamental crowning of spire, tower or buttress.
POPPYHEAD	an ornamental decoration on the tops of bench-ends or stalls and usually in the form of a leaf or flower.

PISCINA	a bowl let into the wall by the altar used to wash the hands and sacred vessels, occasionally found free standing on a pillar.
PRESBYTERY	part of the church where the altar is placed, usually in the east
PULPIT (THREE TIERED)	there were three positions, the lower one was where the parish clerk sat, the middle was where the priest conducted the service and the top one was where he delivered the sermon.
REREDOS	decorated panel above and sometimes all round the altar.
ROOD SCREEN	the screen separating a chapel from the rest of the church often placed between the chancel from the nave.
ROSE WINDOW	circular window, with tracery radiating from the centre.
SADDLEBACK	normal slated pitched roof over a tower.
SEDILIA	seats for priests during long services, usually on the south side of the chancel.
SQUINT	a hole cut in a wall or through a pier to allow a view of the main altar.
STALL	a carved seat or stall.
TRACERY	intersecting ribwork in the upper part of a window, can be used to date the window.
TRANSEPT	transverse section of a cross shaped church, often called the north and south transept.
TYMPANUM	the area between the lintel of a door and the arch above it.
WEEPERS	small figures in niches alongside some medieval tombs.

CHURCH FONTS: *The earliest fonts were not provided with covers, but in the thirteenth century the Archbishop ordered that font covers be provided with some way to lock them. This was usually with an iron strap and a lock thus enabling the baptismal water, which had been blessed to be left in the font. Some people at the time thought that the water contained magical powers. During Cromwell's time many of the covers in churches were forcibly ripped off and the stone font was often damaged.*

SCRATCH DIALS: *In medieval times the scratch dial was the only means of telling the time of day and the population were very dependant on these dials. The medieval dials were mainly circular and the lines were etched in divisions of fifteen degrees. The line which the shadow hit at nine o clock was etched more deeply to signify morning mass and was called the "mass line". The iron which cast the shadow was usually inserted in a hole in the centre of the dial so that on Midsummer's Day the shadow fell across the central line at noon. Some were called "Tide Dials" and had four lines showing when the tides were due. These dials lasted until clocks and railway time tables were introduced. Vertical sundials of the eighteenth century are a feature of most churches. They were usually square with radiating lines at about an hours difference and normally on a south facing wall or over the church doorway. Northamptonshire has over 130 examples of these dials.*
Reproduced by kind permission of Colin Lindsay.

APPENDIX 2

FEATURES TO LOOK FOR IN
AN OLD ENGLISH CHURCH

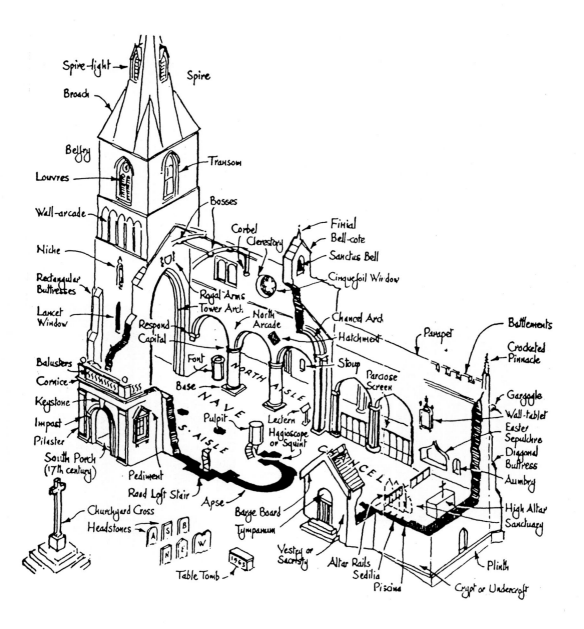

Drawn by Anthony S B New and reproduced by kind permission.

APPENDIX 3

PERIODS OF ENGLISH ARCHITECTURE

Church windows and doors offer strong characteristics of their architectural period. These four illustrations will add interest and help to identify their dates.

ST. GILES, NORTHAMPTON
WEST DOORWAY NORMAN

1066-1889

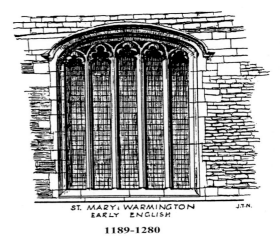

ST. MARY, WARMINGTON
EARLY ENGLISH

1189-1280

MILTON MALSOR: DECORATED

1280-1377

ST. MARY, TITCHMARSH
PERPENDICULAR.

1377-1500

Sketches drawn by John T Neville RIBA, and reproduced by kind permission.

BIBLIOGRAPHY

A Companion to the English Parish Church, Stephen Friar, Sutton
A Wanderer in Northamptonshire, George Harrison, The Mitre Press 1946 (Library ref)
Buildings of England,(Northamptonshire), Nickolas Pevsner, Penguin 1961
Church and Parish (A guide for local historians), J.H.Betty 1987
Churches of the Nene Valley 1880, (Library ref. only)
Exploring Oundle, Ian Bishop, Jema Publications 1995
Exploring Northamptonshire, Tony Noble, Meridian 1989
History of Northamptonshire, Whellan & Co, 1849, (Library ref only)
Northamptorshire, Tony Ireson, Robert Hale
Northamptonshire, Wakeling Dry, Methuen & Co 1913
Northamptonshire and The Soke of Peterborough, Juliet Smith, Shell Guide 1968
The Second Journey, Vera & John Worledge, Meridian 1994
The Kings England (Northamptonshire), Arthur Mee, Hodder & Stoughton 1946
The Northamptonshire Village Book, WI, Countryside Books 1989
Wanderers in Northamptonshire, Vera & John Worledge, Meridian 1992

The church of the **BLESSED VIRGIN MARY, HIGHAM FERRERS**

INDEX

Abthorpe 34
Addington
    Little 84
    Great 84
Adstone 31
Alderton 24
Aldwinkle 87
Apethorpe 81
Arthingworth 57
Ashby St Ledgers 46
Ashley 64
Ashton 21
Aston-le-Walls 41
Aynho 42

Badby 44
Barby 45
Barnwell 83
Barton Seagrave 68
Benefield
    Lower 86
    Upper 86
Blakesley 29
Blatherwycke 74
Blisworth 22
Boddington 30
Boughton 48
Bozeat 99
Brackley 41
Bradden 34
Brafield 97
Brampton Ash 65
Braunston 45
Braybrooke 58
Brigstock 86
Brington
    Great 53
Brixworth 50
Brockhall 47
Broughton 62
Bugbrooke 18
Bulwick 69
Burton Latimer 63
Byfield 29

Caldecote 100
Canons Ashby 31
Catesby 41
Castle Ashby 98
Chacombe 41
Charlton 42
Charwelton 40
Chelveston 100

Chipping Warden 40
Church Brampton 52
Clipston 59
Clopton 79
Cogenhoe 97
Cold Ashby 57
Cold Higham 28
Collingtree 21
Collyweston 73
Corby
    Gt Oakley 69
    Lit Oakley 70
    Old Corby 70
Cosgrove 24
Cottesbrooke 51
Cotterstock 80
Cottingham 70
Courteenhall 20
Cranford 77
Cransley 62
Creaton 51
Crick 55
Croughton 40
Culworth 31

Daventry 44
Deanshanger 39
Deene 68
Denford 85
Denton 97
Desborough 65
Dingley 65
Dodford 47
Draughton 57
Duddington 73

Earls Barton 94
East Carlton 70
Eastern Maudit 99
Easton Neston 23
East Farndon 57
East Haddon 53
Easton on the Hill 74
Ecton 95
Edgecote 39
Everdon 27
Eydon 37

Farthinghoe 38
Farthingstone 27
Fawsley 27
Finedon 94
Flore 18

Fotheringhay 80
Furtho 25

Gayton 19
Geddington 67
Glapthorn 85
Grafton Regis 24
Grafton Underwood 63
Great Doddington 95
Great Oxendon 58
Greatworth 38
Greens Norton 34
Grendon 98
Gretton 69
Guilsborough 54

Hannington 49
Hardwick 93
Hargrave 100
Harlestone 52
Harrington 57
Harringworth 72
Harrowden
    Great 93
    Little 92
Hartwell 21
Haselbech 59
Hellidon 30
Helmdon 38
Hemington 79
Higham Ferrers 90
Hinton-in-the-Hedges 38
Holcot 50
Holdenby 52
Hollowell 54
Horton 20
Houghton
    Great 96
    Little 96
Hulcote 23

Irchester 89
Irthlingborough 92
Isham 92
Islip 84

Kelmarsh 59
Kettering
    Peter & Paul 68
Kilsby 46
Kings Cliffe 73
Kings Sutton 36
Kislingbury 18

Lamport 60
Laxton 69
Lilbourne 56
Litchborough 29
Loddington 62
Long Buckby 55
Lowick 86
Luddington 79
Lutton 79

Maidford 30
Maidwell 60
Marston St Lawrence 37
Marston Trussell 58
Mears Ashby 96
Middleton Cheney 37
Milton Malsor 19
Moreton Pinkney 32
Moulton 50

Naseby 54
Nassington 78
Nether Heyford 18
Newbottle 42
Newnham 44
Newton Bromswold 100
Newton in the Willows 67
Northampton:
    Abington 15
    All Saints 11, 12
    Dallington 15
    Duston 14
    Holy Sep 12
    Kingsthorpe 14
    St Giles 15
    St Matthew's 14
    St Peter's 13
    Weston Favell 15
Norton 47

Oakley
    Great 69
    Little 70
Old 48
Orlingbury 92
Orton 63
Oundle 81
Overstone 96

Passenham 39
Pattishall 22
Paulerspury 23
Piddington 20
Pilton
Pipewell 67

Pitsford 49
Plumpton 36
Polebrook 79
Potterspury 24
Preston Capes 30
Preston Deanery 20, 25
Pytchley 93

Quinton 20

Radstone 36
Raunds 91
Ravensthorpe 54
Ringstead 85
Roade 21
Rockingham 72
Rothersthorpe 19
Rothwell 66
Rushden 91
Rushton 66

Scaldwell 48
Sibbertoft 54
Silverstone 36
Slapton 34
Slipton 78
Southwick 85
Spratton 51
Stanford on Avon 56
Stanion 71
Stanwick 98
Staverton 44
Stoke Albany 65
Stoke Bruerne 22
Stoke Doyle 10, 81
Stowe 28
Strixton 90
Sudborough 77
Sulgrave 32
Sutton Bassett 64
Syresham 35
Sywell 95

Tansor 80
Thenford 36
Tiffield 22
Thornby 51
Thorpe Achurch
Thorpe Malsor 62
Thorpe Mandeville 33
Thrapston 83
Thurning 78
Titchmarsh 82
Towcester 22
Twywell 78

Upton 18

Wadenhoe 82
Wakerley 71
Walgrave 48
Wappenham 33
Warkton 63
Warkworth 36
Warmington 79
Watford 55
Weedon 28
Weedon Lois 33
Weekley 63
Weldon 71
Wellingborough
    All Hallows 89
Welton 46
West Haddon 55
Weston by Welland 64
Whilton 47
Whiston 97
Whitfield 35
Whittlebury 35
Wicken 35
Wilbarston 64
Wilby 89
Winwick 55
Wollaston 89
Woodford 84
Woodford Halse 31
Woodnewton 85
Wootton 21

Yardley Hastings 98
Yarwell 78
Yelvertoft 55